Japan through the World's Eyes

Nina Wegner
Uno Yoko

写真：アフロ、wikipedia 他

p.24 German Federal Archive, p.30 Zhang Zhenshi, p.38 Chris Collins of the Margaret Thatcher Foundation, p.46 Claude TRUONG-NGOC, p.66 Duncan Ralinson, p.72 Steve Jurvetson, p.76 DFID-UK Department for International Development, p.78 World Economic Forum from Cologny, Sweizerland, p.80 Gage Skidmore, p.98 picture alliance/アフロ, p.102 See Li from London, UK, p.116 Tom Palumbo, p.118 Mariusz Kubik, p.122 Kai Kowalewski, p.126 Roy Kerwood, p.130 Zoran Veselinovic, p.132 Sarah Marklund and Hanna Söderlund, p.134 http://www.flickr.com/photos/marcen27/, p.136 compulsiveprep_8, p.140 Ralph Daily, p.144 Gerald Geronimo, p.146 penguin k from North Hollywood, USA, p.148 REX FEATURES/アフロ, p.150 Sound Opinions, p.152 Christopher William Adach from London, UK, p.156 Gdcgraphics at http://flickr.com/photos/gdcgraphics/, p.158 Julien Rath, p.160 MTV Live at http://www.mtv.ca/live, p.164 Steve Jurvetson, p.168 Keith Allison, p.170 Addersolen, p.176 Noelle Neu, p.178 The Heart Truth, p.180 Arturo Pardavila III

装　　幀＝寄藤文平、杉山健太郎

ニッポン
感想記

Japan through the World's Eyes

Nina Wegner
ニーナ・ウェグナー＝著

Uno Yoko
宇野葉子＝訳

まえがき

　世界の人たちが日本のことをどう考えているか知りたいと思ったことはありませんか？　世界の人たちは日本の文化、指導者、価値、歴史をどのように捉えているのでしょう？　もちろん、国によっても人によっても、意見は大きく異なるでしょう。でも、人々が日本と日本人について語った最も注目すべきことにはどんなことがあるのでしょう？

　本書に収録したのは、1世紀を越える歴史のなかで、有名人が日本という国について語った最も忘れがたく、興味深い、そして驚くべきことの一部です。ここには、世界で最も偉大な指導者、芸術家、科学者、音楽家、スポーツ選手、思想家のうちの何人かの考察と感想が述べられています。日本に対するこれらの見解は様々ですが、世界がこの島国をどのように理解しているのか垣間見ることができます。本書を読んで、すべての人が同じ意見ではないことに気づかれるでしょう。フィンセント・ファン・ゴッホのように、日本人は芸術において偉大なことを成し遂げたと信じる人もいれば、パブロ・ピカソのように、日本の芸術作品を好まない人もいます。でも、おそらく、賛成できてもできなくても、どの見解にも何らかの価値があることに気づかれるでしょう。

PREFACE

Have you ever wondered what the rest of the world thinks about your country? How do others see your culture, leaders, values, and history? Of course, opinions may vary wildly from country to country and person to person. But what would be some of the most notable things people have said about Japan and the Japanese?

Collected in this book are some of the most memorable, interesting, and surprising things famous people have said over a century of history about the nation of Japan. Included are the thoughts and impressions of some of the world's greatest leaders, artists, scientists, musicians, athletes, and thinkers. These perspectives on Japan, though very diverse, give us a glimpse into how the world perceives this island nation. You'll see that not everyone agrees. Some, such as Vincent van Gogh, believe the Japanese have achieved great things in art, while others, such as Pablo Picasso, don't care for Japanese artworks. But perhaps you will see some value in every viewpoint, whether you agree or not.

ここに収めた内容は、西洋世界の至るところから集め、私信や日記、インタビューや演説、書物や伝記、公式文書や外交文書などから引用しています。日本に関するこれらの考察を読むことが、読者の皆さまにとって目を見張るような経験になることを願ってやみません。

《読みすすめるにあたって》

　海外の60数名の有名人が、日本をどのように見ているのか訳すにあたって、人数分の知の旅に出かけた気がしました。次にどんな人がどんなことを語るのかと、興味がつきませんでした。

　好意的な意見はうれしいし、辛口の意見にも耳を傾ける必要があります。一番、心に残ったのは、どうして日本は戦争に突入してしまったのかということでした。ガンディーの手紙を日本の軍閥が真摯に受け止めていればと願わずにおれません。クリントン大統領が第二次世界大戦中に強制収容所に収容された日系アメ

These quotes have been gathered from all over the Western world, pulled from personal letters and journals, from interviews and speeches, from books and biographies, from official correspondence and diplomatic communications. We hope that reading these thoughts on Japan will be an eye-opening experience.

リカ人に出した誠実な手紙にも心を打たれました。

　英語と日本語が並ぶ対訳形式になっていますので、見比べて、それぞれの英文がどのように訳されているのかわかるように、なるべく原文の順序にそって訳しています。そのため、少々固い表現になっている箇所もあります。

　著者の前書きにもありますが、本書は私にとっても「目を見張るような経験」でした。読者の皆さまにも、この経験を分かち合っていただければ幸いです。

宇野葉子

目次
Contents

第1章　世界の指導者と軍人 13

マシュー・C・ペリー　*14*　　ウィンストン・チャーチル　*16*
フランクリン・デラノ・ルーズベルト　*20*　アドルフ・ヒトラー　*24*
ダグラス・マッカーサー　*26*　　毛沢東　*30*
ロナルド・レーガン　*32*　　ビル・クリントン　*34*
マーガレット・サッチャー　*38*　ジョージ・H・W・ブッシュ　*40*
バラク・オバマ　*42*　　アウンサンスーチー　*46*
ミシェル・オバマ　*48*

第2章　科学者と知識人 51

アルベルト・アインシュタイン　*52*　バートランド・ラッセル　*56*
モハンダース・カラムチャンド・ガンディー　*58*
ロバート・オッペンハイマー　*62*　ジャン＝ポール・サルトル　*64*
ノーム・チョムスキー　*66*　　スティーヴン・ホーキング　*68*

第3章　ビジネスマンと起業家 71

スティーブ・ジョブズ　*72*　　ビル・ゲイツ　*76*
カルロス・ゴーン　*78*　　ドナルド・トランプ　*80*
J・ポール・ゲティ　*82*

第4章　画家とデザイナー 85

フィンセント・ファン・ゴッホ　*86*　パブロ・ピカソ　*88*
エドガー・ドガ　*90*　　ポール・ゴーギャン　*92*
グスタフ・クリムト　*94*　　フランク・ロイド・ライト　*96*
キース・ヘリング　*98*　　ヴィヴィアン・ウエストウッド　*102*

Chapter 1 **World Leaders and Military Personnel.... 13**

Matthew C. Perry *15*
Franklin Delano Roosevelt *21*
Douglas MacArthur *27*
Ronald Reagan *33*
Margaret Thatcher *39*
Barack Obama *43*
Michelle Obama *49*

Winston Churchill *17*
Adolf Hitler *25*
Mao Zedong *31*
Bill Clinton *35*
George H. W. Bush *41*
Aung San Suu Kyi *47*

Chapter 2 **Scientists and Intellectuals 51**

Albert Einstein *53*
Mohandas Karamchand Gandhi *59*
Robert Oppenheimer *63*
Noam Chomsky *67*

Bertrand Russell *57*
Jean-Paul Sartre *65*
Stephen Hawking *69*

Chapter 3 **Businesspeople and Entrepreneurs....... 71**

Steve Jobs *73*
Carlos Ghosn *79*
J. Paul Getty *83*

Bill Gates *77*
Donald Trump *81*

Chapter 4 **Artists and Designers................... 85**

Vincent van Gogh *87*
Edgar Degas *91*
Gustav Klimt *95*
Keith Haring *99*

Pablo Picaso *89*
Paul Gauguin *93*
Frank Lloyd Wright *97*
Vivienne Westwood *103*

第5章　作家.................................. **105**

ウォルト・ホイットマン　*106*　　オスカー・ワイルド　*108*
ウィリアム・バトラー・イエーツ　*110*　　エズラ・パウンド　*114*
ジャック・ケルアック　*116*　　デイヴィッド・ミッチェル　*118*

第6章　音楽家.................................. **121**

マイルス・デイビス　*122*　　ジョン・レノン　*126*
マイケル・ジャクソン　*130*　　ビヨンセ・ノウルズ　*132*
レディー・ガガ　*134*　　グウェン・ステファニー　*136*
ヨーヨー・マ　*140*

第7章　俳優と映画製作者.................. **143**

スティーヴン・スピルバーグ　*144*　　クエンティン・タランチーノ　*146*
ロマン・コッポラ　*148*　　ロジャー・イーバート　*150*
ビル・マーレイ　*152*　　クリント・イーストウッド　*154*
トミー・リー・ジョーンズ　*156*　　ヒュー・グラント　*158*
トム・クルーズ　*160*　　エドワード・ノートン　*164*

第8章　スポーツ選手とスタッフ............ **167**

デレク・ジーター　*168*
クリスティアーノ・ロナウド・ドス・サントス・アヴェイロ　*170*
モハメド・アリ　*172*　　バリー・ボンズ　*174*
アポロ・オーノ　*176*　　クリスティー・ヤマグチ　*178*
ロブ・マンフレッド　*180*

Chapter 5 Writers 105

Walt Whitman *107*
William Butler Yeats *111*
Jack Kerouac *117*
Oscar Wilde *109*
Ezra Pound *115*
David Mitchell *119*

Chapter 6 Musicians 121

Miles Davis *123*
Michael Jackson *131*
Lady Gaga *135*
Yo-Yo Ma *141*
John Lennon *127*
Beyoncé Knowles *133*
Gwen Stefani *137*

Chapter 7 Actors and Movie Makers 143

Steven Spielberg *145*
Roman Coppola *149*
Bill Murray *153*
Tommy Lee Jones *157*
Tom Cruise *161*
Quentin Tarantino *147*
Roger Ebert *151*
Clint Eastwood *155*
Hugh Grant *159*
Edward Norton *165*

Chapter 8 Athletes and Sports Professionals...... 167

Derek Jeter *169*
Cristiano Ronaldo dos Santos Aveiro *171*
Muhammad Ali *173*
Apolo Ohno *177*
Rob Manfred *181*
Barry Bonds *175*
Kristi Yamaguchi *179*

第1章
世界の指導者と軍人

Chapter 1
World Leaders and Military Personnel

Matthew C. Perry
Winston Churchill
Franklin Delano Roosevelt
Adolf Hitler
Douglas MacArthur
Mao Zedong
Ronald Reagan
Bill Clinton
Margaret Thatcher
George H. W. Bush
Barack Obama
Aung San Suu Kyi
Michelle Obama

マシュー・C・ペリー

マシュー・C・ペリー（1794〜1858）は、アメリカ海軍の提督で、西洋への日本開国において重要な役割を果たしました。日米和親条約（神奈川条約）の交渉責任者を務め、1854年に条約が締結されました。ペリーはアメリカと日本間で調印された条約をまとめるのに威嚇的な方策を取ったことで知られています。ところが、日本と日本国民は提督に深い印象を与えたようで、彼は、日本遠征記録を出版するため、晩年を執筆と準備に費やしました。

「日本人は極度に好奇心が強く、創意工夫に富む我がアメリカ国民による数えきれないほどの発明品を見せられ、この性癖を満たすためのあり余るほどの材料を得たわけである。彼らはこれらの物すべてを綿密に調査しても飽き足らず——彼らにとっては並外れて不思議であったに違いないので——士官や船員のあとをついて回り、あらゆる機会を捉えては士官たちの衣服をくまなく調べた。そして、ボタンを1つでも2つでももらいたいと懇願した。乗船を許された者たちも同様に知識欲旺盛で、目に入るところは隅から隅まで目を凝らし、あれやこれやと計測し、目に留まるものは何でも自己流に写生した。とはいっても、彼らの絵から何を描こうとしているのか見極めるのは困難だっただろう」

——マシュー・C・ペリー提督の日記、1854年ころ

Matthew C. Perry

Matthew C. Perry (1794–1858), a commodore of the United States Navy, played an important role in the opening of Japan to the West. He was the chief negotiator at the Convention of Kanagawa, which took place in 1854. Perry was known to have used intimidation tactics to broker the treaty that was signed between the U.S. and Japan, however, the people and nation of Japan seemed to have impressed the commodore, for he spent his last years writing and preparing for publication an account of his expedition to Japan.

"The Japanese are remarkable for their inordinate curiosity and, in the display of so many of the inventions of our ingenious countrymen, they had ample means of gratifying this propensity. They were not satisfied with the minutest examination of all these things, surpassingly strange as they must have been to them, but followed the officers and men about, seizing upon every occasion to examine every part of their garments, and showing the strongest desire to obtain one or more of their buttons. Those who were admitted on board the ships were equally inquisitive, peering into every nook and corner accessible to them, measuring this and that, and taking sketches after their manner of whatever they could lay their eyes upon, though it would be difficult to discover from their drawings what they were intended to represent."

——Commodore Matthew C. Perry, personal journal, c. 1854

ウィンストン・チャーチル

ウィンストン・チャーチル卿（1874〜1965）は、ノーベル賞を受賞したイギリスの政治指導者で、イギリス首相を2度務めました。戦時期の偉大な指導者とみなされることが多く、第二次世界大戦で連合軍を勝利に導くのに一役買い、アドルフ・ヒトラー政権に終止符を打ちました。日本への宣戦布告は、駐英日本大使への手紙を通して行われました。

「拝啓

12月7日の夜、イギリス国王陛下の政府は、日本軍が、宣戦布告による事前警告、あるいは条件付き宣戦布告を記した最後通牒による事前警告もなく、マレー半島に上陸を企て、シンガポールと香港を爆撃したことを知りました。

Winston Churchill

Sir Winston Churchill (1874–1965) was a Nobel Prize-winning British political leader who served as prime minister of England twice. He is often regarded as a great wartime leader, who helped pave the way for the Allies' victory during World War II and putting an end to the reign of Adolf Hitler. His declaration of war on Japan came via a letter written to the Japanese ambassador to Great Britain, which read as follows:

"Sir,

On the evening of December 7th His Majesty's Government in the United Kingdom learned that Japanese forces without previous warning either in the form of a declaration of war or of an ultimatum with a conditional declaration of war had attempted a landing on the coast of Malaya and bombed Singapore and Hong Kong.

いわれのない侵略というこのような非人道的な行為は、国際法、特に第3回ハーグ陸戦条約の戦争開始に関する第1条に対する重大違反であり、また日本およびイギリスが当条約の加盟国であることを鑑みて、東京在住の国王陛下の大使に、大日本帝国政府に対して、イギリス国王陛下政府の名の下に、両国間が交戦状態に入ったことを告げるように命じました。

敬意を持って
敬具

ウィンストン・S・チャーチル

　　　——ウィンストン・チャーチル、駐英日本大使宛ての手紙、
　　　　1941年12月8日

In view of these wanton acts of unprovoked aggression committed in flagrant violation of International Law and particularly of Article I of the Third Hague Convention relative to the opening of hostilities, to which both Japan and the United Kingdom are parties, His Majesty's Ambassador at Tokyo has been instructed to inform the Imperial Japanese Government in the name of His Majesty's Government in the United Kingdom that a state of war exists between our two countries.

I have the honour to be, with high consideration,
Sir,
Your obedient servant,
Winston S. Churchill"

——Winston Churchill, letter to Japanese ambassador,
December 8, 1941

フランクリン・デラノ・ルーズベルト

フランクリン・デラノ・ルーズベルト（1882～1945）は、1933年から1945年に亡くなるまでアメリカの大統領を務めました。史上初めて大統領選挙を4度勝ち抜き、任期のうち12年間、在職しました。国内では、長期にわたる多くの政策を成功させたことで有名ですが、大半の人の記憶に残っているのは、おそらく1941年にドイツと日本に宣戦布告し、アメリカをその場で第二次世界大戦の連合国に加盟させたことでしょう。

「昨日の1941年12月7日は汚辱の日として残るでしょう。この日にアメリカ合衆国は突然、意図的に、大日本帝国の海軍と空軍に攻撃されました。

合衆国はかの国とは平和的な状態にありました。そして日本の懇願を受けて、日本政府および天皇となお交渉を続け、太平洋の平和維持を目指してきました。

Franklin Delano Roosevelt

Franklin Delano Roosevelt (1882–1945) was the president of the United States from 1933 until his death in 1945. He served as president for twelve years out of a record-setting four terms. He is well known in America for many successful and long-standing policies, but he is perhaps remembered by most for declaring war against Germany and Japan in 1941, leading the U.S. to join the Allies on the ground in World War II.

"Yesterday, December 7th, 1941—a date which will live in infamy—the United States of America was suddenly and deliberately attacked by naval and air forces of the Empire of Japan.

"The United States was at peace with that nation and, at the solicitation of Japan, was still in conversation with its government and its emperor looking toward the maintenance of peace in the Pacific.

日本からハワイまでの距離を考えると、今回の攻撃は数日前、いえ数週間前から周到に計画されたのは明らかだということが、記録に残るでしょう。交渉期間中、日本政府は偽りの声明と平和維持の希望を表明して、合衆国を意図的に欺こうとしました。

　昨日のハワイ諸島への攻撃で、我が国の海軍ならびに軍事力は深刻な損害を被りました。残念なことですが、大勢のアメリカ人の命が失われました。さらに、我が国の艦船がサンフランシスコとホノルルの間の公海において魚雷で爆破されたとの報告も入っています……私は、1941年12月7日、日曜日の、日本によるいわれのない卑怯な攻撃以来、合衆国と大日本帝国が交戦状態に入ったと宣言することを議会に要求します」

――フランクリン・デラノ・ルーズベルト、
「真珠湾攻撃を国民に告げる演説」、1941年12月8日

"It will be recorded that the distance of Hawaii from Japan makes it obvious that the attack was deliberately planned many days or even weeks ago. During the intervening time, the Japanese government has deliberately sought to deceive the United States by false statements and expressions of hope for continued peace.

"The attack yesterday on the Hawaiian Islands has caused severe damage to American naval and military forces. I regret to tell you that very many American lives have been lost. In addition, American ships have been reported torpedoed on the high seas between San Francisco and Honolulu. . . . I ask that the Congress declare that since the unprovoked and dastardly attack by Japan on Sunday, December 7th, 1941, a state of war has existed between the United States and the Japanese empire."

——Franklin Delano Roosevelt, *Pearl Harbor Address to the Nation*,
December 8, 1941

アドルフ・ヒトラー

アドルフ・ヒトラー（1889〜1945）は、現代史のなかで最も悪名高い人物の1人で、ドイツのナチ党の党首として、1933年から1945年までドイツ首相を務めました。彼はホロコースト（ユダヤ人大虐殺）の首謀者で、第二次世界大戦の中心人物でした。

「いいかね、不運にも我々は間違った信仰を持った。何故、日本人と同じ信仰を持たなかったのだ？ 彼らは祖国への犠牲を最高の美徳と考えているじゃないか。イスラム教もキリスト教より、我々に合っていたはずだよ。何故、従順で軟弱なキリスト教でなくてはいけなかったのだい？」

——アドルフ・ヒトラー、オーバーザルツベルクでの非公式な会話、1942年ころ（アルベルト・シュペール著『ナチス狂気の内幕』、サイモン＆シェスター社、1970年、96ページから引用）

Adolf Hitler

Adolf Hitler (1889–1945), one of the most notorious figures of modern history, was the leader of the Nazi Party in Germany and served as the chancellor of Germany from 1933 to 1945. Hitler was the mastermind behind the Holocaust and was a central figure in World War II.

"You see, it's been our misfortune to have the wrong religion. Why didn't we have the religion of the Japanese, who regard sacrifice for the Fatherland as the highest good? The Mohammedan religion too would have been more compatible to us than Christianity. Why did it have to be Christianity with its meekness and flabbiness?"

——Adolf Hitler, in private talks at Obersalzberg, c. 1942 (cited in *Inside the Third Reich* by Albert Speer, New York: Simon and Schuster, 1970, p. 96)

ダグラス・マッカーサー

ダグラス・マッカーサー（1880～1964）は、アメリカの最も偉大な軍事指導者の1人として知られ、アメリカ陸軍の元帥およびフィリピン陸軍の元帥でもありました。第二次世界大戦の太平洋戦域で大活躍し、1945年から1951年まで続いたアメリカの日本占領を指揮しました。

「戦争以来、日本国民は近代史に記録されたなかで最大の改革を経験しました。立派な意志、学ぼうとする熱意、そして際立った理解力で、戦争の焼け跡から、個人の自由と人間の尊厳の優位性を実現するための殿堂を、日本に築き上げました。その後の過程で、政治道徳、経済活動の自由、社会正義の推進に尽力する真に国民を代表する政府が作られたのです。

政治的に、経済的に、そして社会的にも、日本は現在、世界の多くの自由主義国と肩を並べており、二度と世界の

Douglas MacArthur

Considered one of America's greatest military leaders, Douglas MacArthur (1880–1964) was a general of the US Army as well as Field Marshall of the Philippine Army. He was very active in the Pacific theater of World War II and oversaw the U.S. occupation of Japan, which lasted from 1945 to 1951.

"The Japanese people since the war have undergone the greatest reformation recorded in modern history. With a commendable will, eagerness to learn, and marked capacity to understand, they have from the ashes left in war's wake erected in Japan an edifice dedicated to the supremacy of individual liberty and personal dignity and in the ensuing process there has been created a truly representative government committed to the advance of political morality, freedom of economic enterprise, and social justice.

"Politically, economically, and socially Japan is now abreast of many free nations of the earth and will not

信頼を裏切ることはないでしょう。日本がアジアの趨勢に大いに有益な影響を与えられるかどうかは、日本の堂々たる態度で証明されています。そのような態度を持って、前進する歩みを少しも緩めることなく、日本国民は戦争や彼らを外界から取り巻く不安や混乱という最近の難問に立ち向かい、国内で共産主義を取り締まってきました」

——ダグラス・マッカーサー元帥、米国議会での演説、1951年4月19日

again fail the universal trust. That it may be counted upon to wield a profoundly beneficial influence over the course of events in Asia is attested by the magnificent manner in which the Japanese people have met the recent challenge of war, unrest and confusion surrounding them from the outside and checked communism within their own frontiers without the slightest slackening in their forward progress."

——General Douglas MacArthur, Address to Congress, April 19, 1951

毛沢東

毛沢東（1893〜1976）は、中国共産党の創立者で、中国共産党中央委員会主席を1945年から1976年に亡くなるまで務めました。中華人民共和国の建国者でもあります。国共内戦で国民党を打ち破ったのちに政権を取りました。毛が、日本が日中戦争の間に中国を占領していなかったら、この勝利はなかったと語ったことはよく知られています。この戦争は1937年から1945年まで続きました。日本が中国から撤退したあと、毛は新たに築かれた中国の政治体制の最高指導者になりました。

「……大日本帝国陸軍が中国の大半を占領したことによって……解放戦争で勝利できる条件が整った……この点については、日本の軍閥のおかげだと言えよう」

――毛沢東、日本社会党の国会議員に語る、1961年1月24日

Mao Zedong

Mao Zedong (1893–1976) was a founding member of the Communist Party of China and served as the first Chairman of the Central Committee of the Communist Party of China from 1945 until his death in 1976. He is the founder of the People's Republic of China. He came into power after defeating the Kuomintang Nationalists in the Chinese Civil War. Mao has been known to say that this defeat may not have been possible if it hadn't been for the Japanese occupation of China during the Second Sino-Japanese War that took place from 1937 to 1945. After the Japanese left China, Mao stepped in as the supreme leader of China's newly formed political system.

". . . it was because the Japanese Imperial Army had occupied most of China . . . that it created the conditions for our victory in the liberation war . . . and for which I would like to thank the Japanese militarists."

——Mao Zedong to a Japanese Socialist Diet member, January 24, 1961

ロナルド・レーガン

ロナルド・レーガン（1911〜2004）は、第40代アメリカ大統領で、1981年から1989年まで2期にわたって在職しました。供給面からの経済刺激を主張するサプライサイド経済学に基づく政策を取ったことで知られ、外交政策に秀でた大統領としても人々の記憶に残っています。大統領は冷戦の終結、ベルリンの壁の崩壊、ソビエト連邦の崩壊に大きな影響を与えました。1983年に訪日し、国会で演説しました。

「今から12年前、やはり秋の日に、私は初めて日本を訪れました。そして今日も、あの日と同じように、活力、独創力、勤勉の精神が、進歩を求める大きな潮となって、日本中を力強く流れているのを感じます。そして以前と同じように、日本の皆様の類まれな才能に心を打たれています。皆様が、過去の持つ優雅さや美しさを失わずに未来を築いておられるからです」

——ロナルド・レーガン、日本の国会での演説、
1983年11月11日

Ronald Reagan

Ronald Reagan (1911–2004) was the 40th president of the United States. He held office for two terms, from 1981 to 1989, and came to be known for his supply-side economic policies. He is also remembered as a foreign policy president who saw the end of the Cold War, the fall of the Berlin Wall, and the fall of the Soviet Union. In 1983, he traveled to Japan and addressed the Diet.

"It was a dozen years ago on an autumn day like this one that I first visited Japan, and today, as then, I feel energy, initiative, and industry surging through your country in a mighty current for progress. And just as before, I am struck by a unique gift of the Japanese people: You do not build your future at the expense of the grace and beauty of your past."

——Ronald Reagan, Address Before the Japanese Diet in Tokyo, November 11, 1983

ビル・クリントン

ビル・クリントン（1946～）は、第42代アメリカ大統領を1993年から2001年まで務めました。社会福祉政策や、平時行政を主導してアメリカの経済拡大のために多くの業績を上げたことで知られています。クリントンは、第二次世界大戦中に合衆国が運営していた日本人強制収容所に収容されていた日系アメリカ人に、連邦議会と前任大統領が謝罪し賠償金を送っていた仕事を引き継ぎ、1993年に、日系アメリカ人の生存者に大統領として謝罪の手紙を出しました。

「50年以上前、合衆国政府は、あなたや他の多くの日系アメリカ人を不当にも強制収容し、立ち退かせ、あるいは移動させました。今日、あなたの同胞であるアメリカ人に代わって、第二次世界大戦中、不当にも日系アメリカ人やその家族の基本的自由を取り上げた行為に対して心からお詫び申し上げます。

『1988年市民自由法』を制定するなかで、私たちは過去の過ちを認め、このような重大な権利の侵害に耐えてこられた皆様に賠償を申し出ることにいたしました。振り返っ

Bill Clinton

Bill Clinton (1946–) was the 42nd president of the United States, serving from 1993 to 2001. He is remembered for his social welfare policies, as well as leading a peacetime administration that included many achievements in U.S. economic expansion. In 1993, following the work of Congress and previous presidents to apologize and send reparations to Japanese Americans who were interned during World War II in Japanese Internment Camps operating in the U.S., Clinton sent out a presidential letter of apology to Japanese American survivors.

"Over fifty years ago, the United States Government unjustly interned, evacuated, or relocated you and many other Japanese Americans. Today, on behalf of your fellow Americans, I offer a sincere apology to you for the actions that unfairly denied Japanese Americans and their families fundamental liberties during World War II.

In passing the Civil Liberties Act of 1988, we acknowledged the wrongs of the past and offered redress to those who endured such grave injustice. In

て気づいたのは、このような国の行為が人種的偏見、戦時の極度の興奮、政治的な指導力の欠如に深く根ざしていたことです。私たちは過去から学び、1人の国民として、全力を尽くして平等の精神と自由を愛する心を蘇らせなければなりません。力を合わせれば、私たちは自由と正義のある未来をすべての人に保証できるでしょう。あなたとご家族の未来が素晴らしいものでありますよう、心からお祈りいたします。

　ビル・クリントン」

——ビル・クリントン、大統領のお詫びの手紙、1993年10月1日

retrospect, we understand that the nation's actions were rooted deeply in racial prejudice, wartime hysteria, and a lack of political leadership. We must learn from the past and dedicate ourselves as a nation to renewing the spirit of equality and our love of freedom. Together, we can guarantee a future with liberty and justice for all. You and your family have my best wishes for the future.

Bill Clinton"

——Bill Clinton, presidential letter of apology, October 1, 1993

マーガレット・サッチャー

マーガレット・サッチャー（1925〜2013）は、イギリス首相を1979年から1990年まで務めました。初の女性首相で、20世紀で最も長く在職したイギリス首相です。冷戦時代、保守党の党首として、国内と国外で自由市場の経済政策の道を開く原動力になりました。その一環として、国外では当時の日本首相、中曽根康弘と親密な関係を築き、日本との外交関係を強化しました。

「中曽根首相の下で、日本は国際問題でさらに活動的な役割を果たし始めました。ですから、彼が1984年の6月に英国を訪問したときに私が感じたのは、私が相手をしている日本の指導者は、西洋の価値観を理解して共感することができ、正しい方向に経済政策を進める覚悟ができているということでした」

―― マーガレット・サッチャー著『サッチャー回顧録――ダウニング街の日々』、1993年

Margaret Thatcher

Margaret Thatcher (1925–2013) served as prime minister of the United Kingdom from 1979 to 1990. She is the only woman to have held the office, and she was the longest-serving prime minister of the United Kingdom in the 20th century. She was a Conservative leader during the Cold War era who was a powerful force in paving the way for free market economic policies, both at home and abroad, including in her foreign relations with Japan and Japan's prime minister at the time, Yasuhiro Nakasone.

"Under Prime Minister Nakasone, Japan began to play a more active role in international affairs. So, when he made a visit to Britain in June 1984 I felt I was dealing with a Japanese leader who understood and sympathized with Western values and had shown that he was prepared to make steps in the right direction on economic policy."

——Margaret Thatcher, *The Downing Street Years*, 1993

ジョージ・H・W・ブッシュ

ジョージ・H・W・ブッシュ（1924〜）は、アメリカの第41代大統領で、第43代大統領のジョージ・W・ブッシュの父です。ブッシュ・シニアは第二次世界大戦の戦歴があり、1989年から1993年まで大統領を務め、「麻薬戦争」を強化し、湾岸戦争で合衆国を主導したことで知られています。CNNのインタビューで、ブッシュは昭和天皇の葬儀に参列したときのことを語っています。

「結局、私は天皇の葬儀に出席することにしましたが、何人かの国家元首は、過去の日本人による残虐行為を理由に参列しませんでした。私は参列にまったくためらいがありませんでした。それどころか、日本とは強い関係で結ばれているのです。ここで私が象徴的に見ているのは過去ではなく、日本に行くことによって見えてくる現在と未来なのです」

——ジョージ・H・W・ブッシュ、CNNのインタビュー、2003年12月20日

George H. W. Bush

George H. W. Bush (1924–) was the 41st president of the United States and is the father of George W. Bush, who became the 43rd president of the U.S. A veteran of World War II, Bush Senior held office from 1989 to 1993 and is known for intensifying the "War on Drugs" as well as leading the U.S. through the Gulf War. In an interview with CNN, Bush talked about attending Emperor Hirohito's funeral.

"I ended up going to his funeral when several heads of state wouldn't do it because of the brutality of the past. And I had no qualms about it. But we have a strong relationship with Japan. And what I am symbolizing is not the past but the present and the future by going there."

——George H. W. Bush, interview with CNN, December 20, 2003

バラク・オバマ

バラク・オバマ（1961～）は、アメリカの第44代大統領で、初のアフリカ系アメリカ人の大統領でもあります。ハワイで生まれ、子供時代の数年をインドネシアで育ちました。ですから、オバマは大半のアメリカ大統領よりもアジアの文化と暮らしを直接に経験しているのです。2009年に日本を訪れ、自身の「アジアへの軸足移動」政策を紹介する演説をしましたが、演説中、しばらく、少年時代に日本を訪れたときの思い出を語りました。

「日本を再訪することができて、とてもうれしいです。ご存知の方もあるかと思いますが、私は少年だったころ母に連れられて鎌倉を訪れました。そこで私はあの何世紀も前の平和と静穏の象徴——ブロンズの大きな阿弥陀如来像を見上げました。まだ子どもでしたから、私は抹茶アイスクリームのほうに惹かれました。鳩山首相には、昨夜の晩餐会で、子どものころのそのような思い出を分かち合うべくアイスクリームを出してくださったことに感謝いたします。ありがとうございます。しかし私は、故郷を遠く離れた小さなアメリカ人に日本の皆様が示してくださった暖かく親切なもてなしを決して忘れたことはありません。

Barack Obama

Barack Obama (1961–), the 44th president of the United States of America, is also the first African American president of the U.S. Born in Hawaii and raised for part of his childhood in Indonesia, Obama is more personally familiar with Asian culture and daily life than most U.S. presidents. In 2009, Obama traveled to Japan and gave an address that introduced his policy of "Pivot to the East," but he spent some time in his speech reminiscing about a boyhood trip to Japan.

"It is wonderful to be back in Japan. Some of you may be aware that when I was a young boy, my mother brought me to Kamakura, where I looked up at that centuries-old symbol of peace and tranquility—the great bronze Amida Buddha. And as a child, I was more focused on the matcha ice cream. And I want to thank Prime Minister Hatoyama for sharing some of those memories with more ice cream last night at dinner. Thank you very much. But I have never forgotten the warmth and the hospitality that the Japanese people showed a young American far from home.

そして今回もあのときと同じ精神を感じています。鳩山首相の丁重な歓迎に、即位20周年を迎えられた天皇皇后両陛下とお会いする特別な栄誉に、日本の皆様の歓待に、それを感じています。そしてもちろん、私がここに来たのは、小浜市民の皆様に、私の挨拶と感謝の気持ちを伝えるためなのです」

　　　――バラク・オバマ、サントリーホールでの演説、2009年11月14日

"And I feel that same spirit on this visit: In the gracious welcome of Prime Minister Hatoyama. In the extraordinary honor of the meeting with Their Imperial Majesties, the Emperor and Empress, on the 20th anniversary of his ascension to the Chrysanthemum Throne. In the hospitality shown by the Japanese people. And of course, I could not come here without sending my greetings and gratitude to the citizens of Obama, Japan."

——Barack Obama, Remarks at Suntory Hall, November 14, 2009

アウンサンスーチー

アウンサンスーチー（1945～）は、アウンサン将軍の娘です。将軍は「ビルマ建国の父」として知られ、イギリスからビルマ独立を勝ち取り、ビルマ共産党を結成しました。アウンサンスーチーは父の跡を継ぎ、圧政的な軍事政権の時代に、野党第一党である国民民主連盟の活動家および指導者になりました。約15年間の自宅軟禁から解放されたあと、日本をはじめ世界中を旅して演説しました。2013年に訪日したとき、京都大学で男女平等について語りました。

「多くの人がビルマの女性は男性と平等の立場で、性差別はないと考えていますが、これは真実ではありません。でも、日本では性差別がそれほど深刻に捉えられていません。調査と統計によりますと、今日の世界で、日本と韓国において、ある種の大きな性差別が見られます……

性差は本来、主に経済状態によって生まれるというのが真実なら、世界で最も大きな性差が日本と韓国で見られるのはどうしてでしょうか？　それは経済的な要因だけはないからです。社会的な価値も要因となっているからです」

——アウンサンスーチー、京都大学での演説、2013年4月

Aung San Suu Kyi

Aung San Suu Kyi (1945–) is the daughter of General Aung San, who is considered the Father of Modern-day Burma. General Aung San negotiated Burma's independence from Britain and founded the Communist Party of Burma. Aung San Suu Kyi followed in her father's footsteps and became an activist and leader of the main opposition party, the National League for Democracy, during a time of oppressive military control. After her release from approximately fifteen years of house arrest, Aung San Suu Kyi has traveled and talked around the world, including Japan. In 2013 she traveled to Japan and gave a speech about gender equality at Kyoto University.

"There are many who imagine Burmese women are on an equal footing with men and that there is no gender discrimination, although that is not true. But I have to say gender discrimination is not seen to be as great as it is in this country. Research and statistics show Japan and South Korea have some of the greatest gender differences in the world today. . . .

"If it's true that the gender gap is largely economic in nature, why is it that the greatest gender gaps in the world exist in Japan and South Korea? It's not just economic factors. It's social values as well."

——Aung San Suu Kyi, Speech at Kyoto University, April 2013

ミシェル・オバマ

ミシェル・オバマ（1964〜）は、アメリカのファーストレディです。2015年3月に、「レット・ガールズ・ラーン（女子に教育を）」というイニシアチブの立ち上げに伴い、日本の安倍晋三首相に会いました。これは、世界中の女子に教育を受けさせようという運動です。アメリカのファーストレディは首相に会う前に、日本のファーストレディ安倍昭恵と昼食をすませていました。2人のファーストレディは安倍昭恵の経営する居酒屋に行ったのでした。オバマ夫人は安倍首相に、安倍夫人と彼女のレストランに感銘を受けたと伝えました。

「安倍首相、何よりも、とても素晴らしい奥さまをお持ちですね。それにレストランも素敵でした。ですからあなたも行ってみられてはいかがですか。よかったら、今度、私が日本に来たときにご一緒しましょう」

——ミシェル・オバマ、安倍首相への言葉、2015年3月19日

Michelle Obama

In March 2015, First Lady of the United States Michelle Obama (1964–) met with Prime Minister Shinzo Abe of Japan to launch the "Let Girls Learn" initiative, a campaign to increase education for girls around the world. The first lady of the U.S. had lunch with the first lady of Japan, Akie Abe, before she met with the prime minister. The first ladies went to Akie Abe's izakaya, and Ms. Obama told the prime minister that she was impressed with both Ms. Abe and her restaurant.

"Prime Minister, first of all, your wife is an amazing woman. And the restaurant is good, so you have to try it. Maybe the next time I come to visit, you can join us."

——Michelle Obama to Prime Minister Shinzo Abe, March 19, 2015

第2章
科学者と知識人

Chapter 2
Scientists and Intellectuals

Albert Einstein
Bertrand Russell
Mohandas Karamchand Gandhi
Robert Oppenheimer
Jean-Paul Sartre
Noam Chomsky
Stephen Hawking

アルベルト・アインシュタイン

アルベルト・アインシュタイン（1879〜1955）は、20世紀で最も有名な科学者および偉大な思想家の1人です。ノーベル賞受賞者で、理論物理学者として相対性原理を提唱しました。この原理は現代物理学の重要な教義になっています。1922年、訪日して、各地で講演をしました。そのとき、天皇皇后両陛下に会い、2人が生涯変わらず、国と国民を賞賛していることに感銘を受けました。

「山本氏＊から日本への招待を受けたとき、数か月間、長い旅に出ようと、ただちに決心した。自分自身の目で日本を見る機会を失ったら、一生、後悔すると思った。私が日本に招待されたことを知った周りの人たちからは、これまでにないほど羨ましがられた。何故なら、私たちにとって、日本ほど神秘のベールに覆われた国はなかったからだ。

あんなに熱心な歓迎を、生涯受けたことがなかった。たしかに、合衆国を訪れたときも大歓迎された。しかし、日本ではどの国よりも、人々の純粋な心からの誠実さを強く感じた。それは日本人が科学を尊敬しているからだと思

Albert Einstein

Albert Einstein (1879–1955) is one of the best-known scientists and great thinkers of the 20th century. He was a Nobel Prize–winning theoretical physicist who came up with the theory of relativity, which became a major tenet of modern physics. In 1922, Einstein traveled to Japan to give a series of talks. He met the emperor and empress of Japan, and was imprinted with a lifelong admiration for the country and its people.

"When I received Yamamoto's invitation to Japan, I immediately decided to make a long trip that might take several months. I thought, if I let the chance of seeing Japan by my own eyes pass by, I would live to regret it. I had never been more envied than in the moment when the people around me found out that I was invited to Japan. It was because Japan was, for us, a country veiled in the haze of mystery like no other.

"That was the most enthusiastic welcome I have ever received in my life. Indeed, I was very much welcomed also in the United States when I visited there. In Japan, however, I felt the people's genuine, unaffected sincerity

う。私はうれしく、とても幸せな気持ちになった。

　たしかに、日本人は西洋人による知的業績を賞賛し、成功と崇高な理想主義の旗印の下に科学の追求に打ち込んできた。しかし、日本人には自らの美徳を失ったり忘れたりしてほしくない。このような美徳は日本人が西洋世界に出会うずっと前から持っていたもので、例を挙げると、日々の生活で発揮される芸術的な感覚と能力、各個人の持つ質素と謙遜の心、そして純粋で穏やかな日本人の精神などである」

　　　　　　——アルベルト・アインシュタイン、慶応義塾大学への訪問時に
　　　　　　　書かれた随筆、1922年

＊山本実彦：1885-1952　大正から昭和の中頃まで出版活動を行っていた改造社の創業者。アインシュタインの来日招聘に尽力した。

more keenly than in any other country. I assumed it was because the Japanese people respected science. I was delighted and felt extremely happy.

"It is true that the Japanese people admire the intellectual achievements by Westerners and have thrown themselves into the pursuit of science under the banner of success and great idealism. I wish, however, that they do not lose or forget their virtues, which they have kept from long before they met the Western world, such as their artistic sense and ability exercised in their everyday life, the simplicity and modesty expected for individuals, and the pure and calm Japanese soul."

—— Albert Einstein, an essay written during his visit to Keio University, 1922

バートランド・ラッセル

バートランド・ラッセル（1872～1970）は、イギリスの哲学者、数学者、運動家で、ノーベル賞を受賞した作家でもありました。歯に衣着せぬ反戦活動家で、反帝国主義者として知られています。1918年、第一次世界大戦中、アメリカは戦争でイギリスを支援するべきでないと公の場で発言したために、6か月投獄されました。1922年、ラッセルは、中国が発展途上国として世界におよぼすと見られる影響と、中国と日本の関係が果たす重要な役割を検討する書物を執筆しました。

「1867年以来、日本は驚くべき変貌を遂げ、人々は非常に驚いた。しかし、さらに驚くべきは、知識と生活様式のこのような大変化が、宗教と倫理にほとんど変化をもたらさなかったと思われることだ……科学は合理主義に向かう傾向があると考えられているが、日本では科学知識の普及が、ミカド崇拝（天皇崇拝）の著しい強化と同時に起こったのだ。これは、日本の文明開化における最も時代錯誤の特徴である。社会学、社会心理学、政治理論の上で、日本は極めて興味深い国である。成し遂げられた東洋と西洋の統合は、特に風変わりな種類のものである。そこには表面に現れている以上に遥かに東洋的なものが存在するが、国の効率化を目指す西洋的なものは何ひとつ欠けていない」

――バートランド・ラッセル、『中国の問題』、1922年

Bertrand Russell

British philosopher, mathematician, activist, and Nobel Prize–winning writer Bertrand Russell (1872–1970) is known for being an outspoken anti-war activist and anti-imperialist. He was jailed for six months in 1918 during World War I for publicly expressing views that the U.S. should not help Britain in the war. In 1922, Russell wrote a book exploring the possible impacts China would have on the world as a developing country, and how China's relationship with Japan played a significant role.

"The transformation of Japan since 1867 is amazing, and people have been duly amazed by it. But what is still more amazing is that such an immense change in knowledge and in way of life should have brought so little change in religion and ethics. . . . Science is supposed to tend to rationalism; yet the spread of scientific knowledge in Japan has synchronized with a great intensification of Mikado-Worship, the most anachronistic feature in the Japanese civilization. For sociology, for social psychology, and for political theory, Japan is an extraordinarily interesting country. The synthesis of East and West which has been effected is of a most peculiar kind. There is far more of the East than appears on the surface; but there is everything of the West that tends to national efficiency."

——Bertrand Russell, *The Problem of China*, 1922

モハンダース・カラムチャンド・ガンディー

モハンダース・カラムチャンド・ガンディー（1869〜1948）は、マハトマ・ガンディーとも呼ばれ、イギリスによる植民地支配からインドを独立に導いた人物として世界中に知られています。平和的な政治的行動主義の力を証明したことでも世界的に有名です。彼の非暴力の市民的不服従運動への献身は、ネルソン・マンデラやマーティン・ルーサー・キング・ジュニアのような世界の指導者や公民権運動家を鼓舞しました。ガンディーはイギリス同様に日本に対しても、熱烈な反帝国主義者で、1942年、日本の軍閥に向けて文書を書き、中国侵略を止め、帝国主義の野望を捨てるように促しました。

「まず始めに、私はあなた方を悪く思ってはいませんが、あなた方の中国への攻撃を激しく嫌悪していると、打ち明けなくてはなりません。あなた方は高尚な高みから降りて帝国主義の野望を持つにいたりました。あなた方はその野望を実現できないばかりか、アジア分割の張本人になるかもしれません。そうすることで、図らずも世界の連合と兄弟愛を妨げることになるのです。これらなしには人類の希望はありません。

Mohandas Karamchand Gandhi

Known internationally as the man who brought about Indian independence from British colonial rule, Mohandas Karamchand Gandhi (1869–1948), also known as Mahatma Gandhi, is world-famous for proving the power of peaceful political activism. His commitment to nonviolent civil disobedience has inspired world leaders and civil rights activists such as Nelson Mandela and Martin Luther King, Jr. Gandhi was a passionate anti-imperialist, as much as it applied to Japan as the United Kingdom. In 1942, he wrote an article addressed to the militarists of Japan that urged them to stop their invasion of China and their imperialist aspirations.

"I must confess at the outset that, though I have no ill-will against you, I intensely dislike your attack upon China. From your lofty height you have descended to imperial ambition. You will fail to realize that ambition and may become the authors of the dismemberment of Asia, thus unwittingly preventing world federation and brotherhood without which there can be no hope for humanity.

50年以上前、私は18歳の若者で、ロンドンで勉学に励んでいました。それ以来、故サー・エドウィン・アーノルド＊の書物から、あなた方の国の多くの優れた特性を尊ぶことを学んできました。南アフリカにいたとき、ロシア軍に対する（日本の）見事な勝利を聞いて興奮しました。1915年に南アフリカからインドに戻ったあと、私は日本の僧侶たちと親しくなりました。彼らは時々、私たちの僧院の一員として暮らしていました。そのなかの1人の僧侶が、セバグラムの僧院の大切な一員になりました。務めに対する彼の専心、威厳のある態度、日々の祈りでの尽きることのない信心……そして心の平安を示す自然な微笑で、彼は私たちみんなに愛されていました。それなのに、日本がイギリスに宣戦布告したために、彼は私たちから引き離され、私たちは仲間を失って寂しい思いをしています。彼が記念に残した毎日の祈りの言葉と小さな太鼓の伴奏に合わせて、私たちは朝夕の祈りを始めています。

　日本の僧侶たちとのこのような楽しい思い出がありますので、私から見れば日本による中国に対するいわれのない攻撃と、また報告が確かだとしたら、あなた方がかの偉大な古代の国で行っている残酷な破壊行為について考えるたびに、深い悲しみに襲われるのです」

　　　　　——M・K・ガンディー、日本の軍閥への文書、1942年7月

＊サー・エドウィン・アーノルド：イギリス出身の日本研究家、仏教学者。
　釈迦の生涯と教えをとく「アジアの光」を刊行した。

"Ever since I was a lad of eighteen studying in London over fifty years ago, I learnt, through the writings of the late Sir Edwin Arnold, to prize the many excellent qualities of your nation. I was thrilled when in South Africa I learnt of [Japan's] brilliant victory over Russian arms. After my return to India from South Africa in 1915, I came in close touch with Japanese monks who lived as members of our Ashram from time to time. One of them became a valuable member of the Ashram in Sevagram, and his application to duty, his dignified bearing, his unfailing devotion to daily worship . . . and his natural smile which was positive evidence of his inner peace had endeared him to all of us. And now that owing to your declaration of war against Great Britain he has been taken away from us, we miss him as a dear co-worker. He has left behind him as a memory his daily prayer and his little drum, to the accompaniment of which we open our morning and evening prayers.

"In the background of these pleasant recollections I grieve deeply as I contemplate what appears to me to be your unprovoked attack against China and, if reports are to believed, your merciless devastation of that great and ancient land."

——M. K. Gandhi, an article addressed to Japanese militarists, July 1942

ロバート・オッペンハイマー

ロバート・オッペンハイマー（1904〜1967）は、原子爆弾を作ったことで最もよく記憶されています。アメリカの理論物理学者のオッペンハイマーは、優れた科学者たちとマンハッタン計画に取り組み、第二次世界大戦中に原子爆弾を造りました。原子物理学への彼の貢献は、科学の大きな進歩と考えられていますが、彼はその後の人生を、科学に付き物の道徳の問題に苦しんで過ごしました。人生の終わりに近づいたとき、オッペンハイマーは原爆が使用された過程を考え直して語りました。

「私は爆弾を造ったことやトリニティ（最初の原爆実験）について、何の後悔もしていません。爆弾の製造や実験は正しく実行されました。爆弾の使用については、どうしてそのようなことが起こったのか理解し、一緒に働いた仲間たちがどのような高潔な気持ちで決定を下したのか認識しています。それにもかかわらず、私にはそれが正しく行われたとは思えません。日本への最後通牒（日本に降伏を要求したポツダム宣言）は偽善的な文句が並べたてられていました……我々の政府はもっと前途の見通しを持って、もっと明瞭に、世界と日本に原子爆弾が何を意味するのか知らせるべきでした」

——ロバート・オッペンハイマー、ランジング・ラモントとのインタビュー、1965年

Robert Oppenheimer

Robert Oppenheimer (1904–1967) is best remembered as the creator of the atom bomb. An American theoretical physicist, Oppenheimer worked on the Manhattan Project with other leading scientists to develop the atom bomb during World War II. Although his contributions to nuclear physics are considered to be major advances in science, Oppenheimer spent the rest of his life struggling with questions of morality as it pertains to science. Near the end of his life, Oppenheimer expressed second thoughts about the way that the atomic bomb was used.

"I have no remorse about the making of the bomb and Trinity [the first test of an atom bomb]. That was done right. As for how we used it, I understand why it happened and appreciate with what nobility those men with whom I'd worked made their decision. But I do not have the feeling that it was done right. The ultimatum to Japan [the Potsdam Proclamation demanding Japan's surrender] was full of pious platitudes . . . our government should have acted with more foresight and clarity in telling the world and Japan what the bomb meant."

——Robert Oppenheimer, in an interview with author Lansing Lamont, 1965

ジャン゠ポール・サルトル

ジャン゠ポール・サルトル（1905〜1980）は、フランスの哲学者、小説家、劇作家で、熱烈な政治活動家でした。1964年、ノーベル文学賞に選ばれましたが、受賞を拒否したことで有名です。日本の哲学界とも親交があり、1966年、同じ哲学者で作家のシモーヌ・ド・ボーヴォワール*と日本を訪れました。旅行中、彼は日本の文化、美学、哲学をほめたたえました。

「日本の家は自然と溶け合っています。家と自然が一体化しているのです。ヨーロッパでは、石の建物が障壁を作っています」

——ジャン゠ポール・サルトル、ジャン・ホーケンソン著『日本、フランス、東西間の美学：フランス文学（1867〜2000）』の、1966年ころより引用

*シモーヌ・ド・ボーヴォワール：サルトルの事実上の妻で、フランスの作家、哲学者。

Jean-Paul Sartre

Jean-Paul Sartre (1905–1980) was a French philosopher, novelist, and playwright, as well as an impassioned political activist. Sartre was awarded the Nobel Prize for Literature in 1964, but he famously refused to accept it. He was involved with the philosophy scene in Japan and came on a tour of Japan with fellow philosopher and writer, Simone de Beauvoir in 1966. During his tour, he expressed his admiration for Japanese culture, aesthetic, and philosophy.

"The Japanese house blends with nature. There is a real cohesion between nature and homes. In Europe, the stone buildings form a barrier."

——Jean-Paul Sartre, quoted c. 1966 in *Japan, France, and East-West Aesthetics: French Literature, 1867–2000*, by Jan Hokenson

ノーム・チョムスキー

ノーム・チョムスキー（1928〜）は、アメリカの知識人で、おそらく、哲学、言語学、社会正義における貢献で最も知られているでしょう。歯に衣着せぬ発言をし、彼が述べた意見が物議をかもすことがしばしばあります。しかし、積極的に文化、政治、歴史、哲学に関する公開の対談に常に参加してきました。現在、マサチューセッツ工科大学の名誉教授を務めています。

「そうです、暴力はときには良いことにつながることがあります。日本が真珠湾を攻撃したことで、良いことがたくさん起きました。跡をたどっていけば、アジアからヨーロッパ人をけちらしたことがわかります——このことでインドだけでも何千万もの命が助かったのです」

——ノーム・チョムスキー、マサチューセッツ工科大学の学生への講義、
『ニューヨーカー』から引用、2003年

Noam Chomsky

Noam Chomsky (1928–) is an American intellectual perhaps best known for his contributions to philosophy, linguistics, and social justice. He is outspoken and often expresses controversial opinions, but has always actively participated in open dialogue about culture, politics, history, and philosophy. He holds the position of Professor Emeritus at the Massachusetts Institute of Technology.

"Yes, sometimes violence does lead to good things. The Japanese bombing of Pearl Harbor led to many very good things. If you follow the trail, it led to kicking Europeans out of Asia—that saved tens of millions of lives in India alone."

——Noam Chomsky to a class of MIT students, quoted in *The New Yorker*, 2003

スティーヴン・ホーキング

スティーヴン・ホーキング（1942 〜）は、存命中の科学者のなかで、おそらく世界で最も有名でしょう。イギリスの理論物理学者、宇宙論者、ケンブリッジ大学の研究者で、彼の著作は世界で広く読まれています。ホーキングは変性疾患、ALS（筋委縮性側索硬化症）と診断されました。長年の間に少しずつ体が麻痺する病気です。『ニューヨークタイムズ』紙のインタビューで、人間の精神の回復力と、この回復力が2011年の東日本大震災後の日本人をどのように救うことができるのか、語っています。

―地球上は、この数か月、まさに壊滅的な状態でした。地震、革命、反革命、それに日本の炉心溶融の記事を読まれて、どのように感じられましたか？　私たちと同じように個人的に動揺されましたか？

「私は数回、日本を訪ねたことがあり、そのたびに暖かい歓待を受けました。このような大惨事にあった日本の同僚や友人のことを思って、深い悲しみを覚えています。日本の復活を支援する世界的な取り組みがあればよいと願っています。私たちは、『1つの種』として、多くの自然災害や困難な状況を乗り越えてきました。ですから、人間の精神は過酷な苦難に耐えられると信じています」

――スティーヴン・ホーキング、『ニューヨークタイムズ』紙のインタビュー、
2011年5月9日

Stephen Hawking

Stephen Hawking (1942–) is perhaps the world's best-known scientist currently alive. He is a British theoretical physicist, cosmologist, and researcher at Cambridge University, as well as a widely read author. Hawking was diagnosed with a degenerative disease, amyotrophic lateral sclerosis (ALS), that has paralyzed him little by little over the years. In a *New York Times* interview, Hawking spoke about the resilience of the human spirit, and how this resilience might help the people of Japan after the 2011 Tohoku earthquake and tsunami.

—Here on Earth, the last few months have just been devastating. What were your feelings as you read of earthquakes, revolutions, counter-revolutions and nuclear meltdowns in Japan? Have you been as personally shaken up as the rest of us?

"I have visited Japan several times and have always been shown wonderful hospitality. I am deeply saddened for my Japanese colleagues and friends, who have suffered such a catastrophic event. I hope there will be a global effort to help Japan recover. We, as a species, have survived many natural disasters and difficult situations, and I know that the human spirit is capable of enduring terrible hardships."

——Stephen Hawking, interview with the *New York Times*, May 9, 2011

第3章
ビジネスマンと起業家

Chapter 3
Businesspeople and Entrepreneurs

Steve Jobs
Bill Gates
Carlos Ghosn
Donald Trump
J. Paul Getty

スティーブ・ジョブズ

スティーブ・ジョブズ（1955～2011）は、アップル社の共同設立者でCEO（最高経営責任者）でしたが、日本を愛したことで知られています。生涯、禅を実践し、たびたび京都を訪れ、取締役会をカリフォルニア州、メンローパークにあるお気に入りの寿司店で開くことさえありました。天才的な発明家で技術設計者として知られたジョブズは、パーソナル・コンピュータの発展に途方もなく大きな影響を与えました。その影響は彼が2011年に癌と闘って亡くなったあと、今日でも感じることができます。

「日本はとても面白い国だ。日本人は真似をしているという人もいるけれど、ぼくはまったくそんな風に思わない。日本人は物を再発明していると思っている。すでに発明された物を手に入れると、それを研究して完全に理解しようとする。場合によっては、元の発明者より深く理解している。そうやって理解してから、彼らはもっと洗練された第二世代バージョンとして再発明するんだ。この戦略が有効なのは、彼らが取り組んでいる物がそれほど大きく変化しない場合に限られる——ステレオ業界や自動車業界はその2例だね。対象物の変化が速いと、彼らはそれを扱うのは困難だと考える。何故なら、そういった物の再発明を完了するのに2、3年は必要だからだ。

Steve Jobs

Steve Jobs (1955–2011), the cofounder and CEO of Apple Inc., was known for his love affair with Japan. He was a lifelong practitioner of Zen Buddhism, a frequent visitor to Kyoto, and even conducted board meetings at his favorite sushi restaurant in Menlo Park, California. Considered a genius inventor and technology designer, Jobs had a tremendous influence on the evolution of personal computers, which continues to be felt today, even after he lost his battle with cancer in 2011.

"Japan's very interesting. Some people think it copies things. I don't think that anymore. I think what they do is reinvent things. They will get something that's already been invented and study it until they thoroughly understand it. In some cases, they understand it better than the original inventor. Out of that understanding, they will reinvent it in a more refined second-generation version. That strategy works only when what they're working with isn't changing very much—the stereo industry and the automobile industry are two examples. When the target is moving quickly, they find it very difficult, because that reinvention cycle takes a few years.

パーソナル・コンピュータの定義が今と同じ速度で変わり続ける限り、日本人はとても苦労するだろう。いったん変化の速度が落ちると、彼らはコンピュータ市場に全力を集中するだろう。何故なら、心底、コンピュータ事業を支配したいからだ。そのことに間違いはない。国家の優先課題だとみなしているからね。

　４、５年もすれば、ようやく日本人はまともなコンピュータの製造方法を突き止めるだろう。アメリカ主導のコンピュータ業界を維持したいなら、我々が世界水準の製造者になるのに、４年しか残されていないということだ。我々の製造技術は日本の技術と同じか超えていなければならないんだ」

　　　　　——スティーブ・ジョブズ、『プレイボーイ』誌のインタビュー、
　　　　　　1985年2月

"As long as the definition of what a personal computer is keeps changing at the rate that it is, they will have a very hard time. Once the rate of change slows down, the Japanese will bring all of their strengths to bear on this market, because they absolutely want to dominate the computer business; there's no question about that. They see that as a national priority.

"We think that in four to five years, the Japanese will finally figure out how to build a decent computer. And if we're going to keep this industry one in which America leads, we have four years to become world-class manufacturers. Our manufacturing technology has to equal or surpass that of the Japanese."

——Steve Jobs, interview with *Playboy*, February 1985

ビル・ゲイツ

ビル・ゲイツ（1955〜）は、世界で最も裕福な人の1人で、発明家、コンピュータ・プログラマー、起業家、実業家、そしてマイクロソフトの共同創設者です。世界で最も成功した起業家の1人として、しばしば技術や事業の開発法を、国レベルで助言しています。2015年前半に、中国で情報技術事業を築くための方法を助言しました。

「注意しないといけないのは、政府がイノベーションに対してどのような姿勢を取るかということです。例えば日本では、いくつかの具体的なイノベーションの目標とアプローチが定められました。いわゆる『第五世代コンピュータ・プロジェクト』ですね。ですがこのやり方は間違っていたわけです……1980年代、アメリカが感じていたのは、『たしかに、日本は我々より優れているし、我々より物を改善する方法を知っているし、政府を巻き込む方法を知っている。それに日本のテレビは我々の物より優秀だ』ということでした。実は1980年代はアメリカにとってとても良い時期だったのです……アメリカ政府がコンピュータ・サイエンスに取り組んだ方法というのは、何十もの異なるアプローチを後押ししたり、競技会を開いたりすることでした。私がお勧めしたいのは、日本と同じ方法を取らないこと、そしてどうしてアメリカのモデルがうまくいったのか考えてみることです」

——ビル・ゲイツ、中国海南省での「2015年ボアオ・アジアフォーラム」で語る、2015年3月

Bill Gates

Bill Gates (1955–), one of the world's wealthiest people, is an inventor, computer programmer, entrepreneur, businessman, and the cofounder of Microsoft. As one of the world's most successful entrepreneurs, he often gives advice on how to develop technology and business on the national level. In early 2015, he advised China on steps to take for building its information technology industry.

"You have to be careful how you structure the government's relationship with innovation. In Japan, they picked some very specific goals and approaches for their so-called 'Fifth General Project'. It was the wrong way to go. . . . In the 1980s, the U.S. was feeling like 'OK, Japan is better than us, they know how to make things better than us, they know how to plan the government, their television is better than us.' And actually it was a very good period for the U.S. . . . The way [the U.S. government] did the computer science stuff was backing dozens and dozens of different approaches and having contests. I would recommend not doing what Japan did and looking at why the U.S. model ended up the best."

——Bill Gates, speaking at the 2015 Boao Forum in Hainan, China, March 2015

カルロス・ゴーン

カルロス・ゴーン（1954〜）は、ルノーのCEO（最高経営責任者）であり日産のCEOでもあります。また、「ルノー・日産アライアンス」の社長とCEOを兼ねています。2002年、『フォーチュン』誌に「アジア・ビジネスマン・オブ・ザ・イヤー」に選ばれ、2003年には同誌より「アメリカ国外にいる10人の最強の事業家の1人」に指名されました。ゴーンはフランスとレバノンとブラジルの多重国籍を有し、ブラジル、フランス、日本で交互に暮らしています。

「日本人は通常、とても用心深く、たとえ変化が必要だと確信していてもその態度をくずしません。これまでに適切な（手段が）取られたか確かめたがります——問題に取り組むのに、手段が過度にではなく、ちょうど必要なだけ取られたか確かめたがるのです。

——カルロス・ゴーン、『ブルームバーグ・ビジネス』誌のインタビュー、2002年

Carlos Ghosn

Carlos Ghosn (1954–) is the CEO of Renault and the CEO of Nissan, as well as chairman and CEO of the Renault-Nissan Alliance. In 2002, *Fortune* magazine named him the Asia Businessman of the Year, and in 2003, he was named one of the top ten most powerful people conducting business outside the U.S. Ghosn is French-Lebanese-Brazilian and lives alternately in Brazil, France, and Japan.

"The Japanese people are usually very prudent, even when they are convinced change is necessary. They want to make sure that the appropriate steps have been taken—that [they're] not too much but enough to address the issue."

——Carlos Ghosn, interview with *Bloomberg Business*, 2002

ドナルド・トランプ

ドナルド・トランプ (1946〜) は、世界で最も顔の知られた投資家および億万長者の1人で、これまでと同様に、おそらく今後もアメリカ大統領の座を狙い続けるでしょう。彼は握手をするという西洋の習慣を嫌悪していることで有名です。そのため、大統領選挙戦でもいくつかの問題が起こりました。

「こんな質問が出ているんだ。『握手しないで、ドナルド・トランプはどうやって選挙を戦うつもりだ？』ってね。実は、長年にわたって、何度も握手をしているし、握手することに抵抗はない。しかし、あれは健康的ではないね。病原菌に関して言えば、『感染するかもしれない』という問題ではない——感染は証明されていて、事実、風邪をうつされるじゃないか。面倒なことになるじゃないか。正直言って、日本の習慣のほうがはるかに賢明だね」

——ドナルド・トランプ、『ローリング・ストーン』誌のインタビュー、2011年5月

Donald Trump

Donald Trump (1946–), one of the world's most recognizable investors and billionaires, has been and perhaps will continue to be a contender for the seat of U.S. President. He is well known for disliking the Western custom of shaking hands, which has caused some troubles in his presidential campaign.

"The question has come out, 'How can Donald Trump campaign if he doesn't shake hands?' Well, over the years, I've shaken many hands, and I have no problem shaking hands. But it's not a healthy thing. With the germs, it's not a question of 'maybe'—they have been proven, you catch colds. You catch problems. Frankly, the Japanese custom is a lot smarter."

——Donald Trump, interview with *Rolling Stone*, May 2011

J・ポール・ゲティ

J・ポール・ゲティ（1892〜1976）は、アメリカの実業家および工業家で、ゲティ・オイル社を創設しました。根っからの美術愛好家で収集家でもあり、ゲティと名のつく美術館、基金、財団を遺産として残しました。1957年には存命する最も裕福なアメリカ人に選ばれ、1996年にはこれまでで最も裕福なアメリカ人の67位にランクされました。

「日本にいたとき、日本人の丁寧な態度、勤勉な性質、誠実さに大いに感銘を受けた。このような日本を知っていたことは、数十年後、ゲティ社が日本企業と多くの商取引を始めたときに、まさに実際的な面で非常に貴重であることがわかった」

——J・ポール・ゲティ、『石油王への道：世界一の富豪 J.ポール・ゲティ回顧録』、1976年

J. Paul Getty

J. Paul Getty (1892–1976) was an American businessman and industrialist who founded the Getty Oil Company. As a great art lover and collector, he has left a legacy of art museums, trusts, and foundations carrying the Getty name. In 1957, J. Paul Getty was named the richest living American, and in 1996, he was ranked the 67th richest American who ever lived.

"In Japan, I was immensely impressed by the politeness, industrious nature and conscientiousness of the Japanese people. Decades later, this acquaintance with Japan was to prove invaluable at a strictly practical level when Getty companies entered into many business transactions with Japanese firms."

——J. Paul Getty, *As I See It: The Autobiography of J. Paul Getty*, 1976

第4章
画家とデザイナー

Chapter 4
Artists and Designers

Vincent van Gogh
Pablo Picasso
Edgar Degas
Paul Gauguin
Gustav Klimt
Frank Lloyd Wright
Keith Haring
Vivienne Westwood

フィンセント・ファン・ゴッホ

フィンセント・ファン・ゴッホ（1853 〜 1890）は、印象派と後期印象派のなかで、おそらく最も有名な画家で、日本画の熱心な収集家でした。日本の美的感覚に感銘して影響を受け、習作としてしばしば浮世絵を模写しました。ゴッホは日本に来たことはありませんが、死を迎えるころには何百枚もの浮世絵を集めていました。代表作のうちの数作品は、日本画を模写したか、それに敬意を表したものです。

「ぼくのすべての作品は、ある程度日本の芸術が基になっている……」

——フィンセント・ファン・ゴッホ、弟テオ・ファン・ゴッホへの手紙、
1888年7月15日

「極度に整然として明瞭な絵を描く日本人が羨ましい。絵はけっして退屈ではなく、けっして急いで仕上げられたようには見えない。彼らの作品は息をするように自然で、人物を数筆で描き、まるでチョッキにボタンをかけるように簡単にやってのける。ああ、ぼくも数筆で人物を描ければいいのに」

——フィンセント・ファン・ゴッホ、弟テオ・ファン・ゴッホへの手紙、
1888年9月24日

Vincent van Gogh

Vincent van Gogh (1853–1890), perhaps the most famous of the Impressionist and Post-Impressionist painters, was an avid collector of Japanese prints. He was inspired and influenced by Japanese aestheticism and often copied ukiyo-e prints as studies. Although van Gogh never traveled to Japan, by the time of his death he had collected hundreds of ukiyo-e, and some of his best-known works are copies of or homages to Japanese art.

1887年、ゴッホの「タンギー爺さん」。
背景には浮世絵が描かれている。

"All my work is based to some extent on Japanese art …"

——Vincent van Gogh, in a letter to his brother, Theo van Gogh, July 15, 1888

"I envy the Japanese for the extreme neatness and clarity in their work. It is never tedious and never seems to be done in a hurry. Their work is as simple as breathing, and they draw a figure with a few sure strokes, as if it were as easy as buttoning a waistcoat. Oh, if only I could draw a figure with just a few lines."

—Vincent van Gogh, in a letter to his brother, Theo van Gogh, September 24, 1888

パブロ・ピカソ

パブロ・ピカソ（1881 〜 1973）は、スペインの芸術家で、キュビズムの創始者と知られ、20世紀で最も影響力のある芸術家の1人としても知られています。ひんぱんに世界中の芸術品を研究して、特にアフリカの芸術に感銘を受けましたが、同時代の芸術家とは異なり、アジアの芸術を好みませんでした。

「わたしは中国、日本、それにペルシャの芸術を好きになったことがない」

——パブロ・ピカソ、1917年ころ、『原始主義と20世紀の芸術：資料による歴史』、ジャック・D・フロムおよびミリアム・ドイチェ編

Pablo Picasso

Pablo Picasso (1881–1973), a Spanish artist that is considered the Father of Cubism, is also considered one of the most influential artists of the 20th century. Although he often studied artwork from around the world and was particularly impressed with African art, he was unlike many of his contemporaries in that he did not prefer Asian art.

"I have never liked the art of China, Japan, or Persia."

——Pablo Picasso, c. 1917, as printed in *Primitivism and Twentieth-century Art: A Documentary History*, edited by Jack D. Flam and Miriam Deutch

エドガー・ドガ

エドガー・ドガ（1834 〜 1917）は、フランスの画家および彫刻家で、印象派の他の多くの芸術家と同じように、日本の浮世絵を賞賛して収集し、いつも研究していました。彼はあまりにも日本の美学に心酔していたので、ある日、若い日本の芸術家に、なぜわざわざフランスの最も名高い芸術学校、エコール・デ・ボザールに入学したのか尋ねました。

「幸運にも日本に生まれたのに、どうしてここ（エコール・デ・ボザール）まで来て、教授たちの厳しい訓練を受けているのかね……？」

——エドガー・ドガ、若い日本の画学生に対して、
ポール・ラフォンド著『ドガ』第1巻148ページより引用

Edgar Degas

Like many other Impressionist artists, French painter and sculptor Edgar Degas (1834–1917) admired and collected Japanese ukiyo-e prints, habitually studying them. He admired the Japanese aesthetic so much that one day, he asked a young Japanese artist why he bothered to enroll at France's most prestigious art school, the École des Beaux-Arts.

"When one has the good fortune of being born in Japan, why come here [the École des Beaux-Arts] to subject oneself to the discipline of professors…?"

——Edgar Degas, to a young Japanese art student, quoted in Paul Lafond's *Degas*, vol. 1, p. 148

ポール・ゴーギャン

ポール・ゴーギャン（1848〜1903）は、フランスの画家で後期印象派として有名ですが、やはり「ジャポニスム」運動の影響を受けました。この運動は1800年代半ばから後半までヨーロッパ芸術界で急速に広まっていました。ゴーギャンは画家、彫刻家、作家、陶芸家、そして木版画家でもありました。多作な芸術家でしたが、世界的な名声を得たのは死後でした。

「北斎は自由に描いている。自由に描くというのは自分に嘘をつかないことだ」

――ポール・ゴーギャン、日記より、『ゴーギャン私記』（ヴァン・ワイク・ブルックス訳）23〜24ページに転載

Paul Gauguin

Paul Gauguin (1848–1903), a French painter who became famous as a Post-Impressionist, was also influenced by the "Japonisme" movement that swept through the European art scene in the mid to late 1800s. Gauguin painted, sculpted, wrote, made pottery, and created wood-block prints. Although Gauguin was a prolific artist, he did not achieve worldwide fame until after his death.

"Hokusai draws freely. To draw freely is not to lie to oneself."

——Paul Gauguin, from a personal journal, reprinted in *Gauguin's Intimate Journals*, translated by Van Wyck Brooks, pp. 23–24

グスタフ・クリムト

グスタフ・クリムト（1862～1918）は、オーストリアの画家で、代表作は『接吻』のような「黄金様式」の作品です。日本の芸術、特に浮世絵の影響を強く受けました。来日したことはありませんが、絶えず日本芸術を研究することで、日本や日本の芸術家を想像の世界でひんぱんに訪れました。

「ときどき、ぼくは午前中の絵の授業をすっぽかして、代わりに公然と日本の書物を研究しています」

――グスタフ・クリムト、恋人のマリー（ミッツィ）・ツィマーマンへの手紙、1903年

Gustav Klimt

Gustav Klimt (1862–1918), an Austrian painter who is best known for his "golden phase" works, such as "The Kiss," was greatly influenced by Japanese art, especially ukiyo-e. Although he never traveled to Japan, he often visited the country and its artists through his imagination, in his constant study of Japanese art.

"Sometimes I miss out the morning's painting session and instead study my Japanese books in the open."

——Gustav Klimt, letter to his lover, Marie (Mizzi) Zimmermann, 1903

クリムトの代表作「接吻」(1908年)

フランク・ロイド・ライト

フランク・ロイド・ライト（1867～1959）は、1991年に米国建築家協会によって「史上最高のアメリカ人建築家」に選ばれました。彼は532の建物を建て、さらに紙の上では500を超える建物を設計しました。自然と一体化した建物の良さを認め、「有機的建物」という新語を作りました。日本の設計や芸術を高く評価したことで知られ、長年にわたり、日本の木版画を集め販売しました。

「有機的な感覚は、建築家にとってなくてはならないものです。自然が与えてくれる実例を尊ぶという流儀以上にその感覚を確実に育めるところがあるでしょうか？……日本の芸術は、ほかのどんな流儀よりもこの流儀と密接に結びついています。日本で一般に使われている言葉に『枝振り』というような言葉が多くあります。これをできるだけ近い言葉に言い換えると、張り出した木の枝の配置という意味になります。英語にこのような言葉がないのは、このような語を考え出すほど私たちは洗練されていないからです。しかし、建築家はこのような言葉で考えるだけでなく、自力で自分の語彙を作り、それと同じくらい意義深い有用な言葉をいくつか、包括的な方法でその語彙に添えることを、この流儀で学ばなければなりません」

——フランク・ロイド・ライト、「建築のために」、『アーキテクチュアル・リコード』誌より、1908年

Frank Lloyd Wright

In 1991, Frank Lloyd Wright (1867–1959) was named "the greatest American architect of all time" by the American Institute of Architects. He built 532 buildings and designed some 500 more on paper. He believed in buildings that blended seamlessly with nature and coined the term "organic architecture." He is known to have had a great admiration for Japanese design and art, and collected and sold Japanese woodblock prints for many years.

ライトが設計した帝国ホテルライト館の正面。

"A sense of the organic is indispensable to an architect; where can he develop it so surely as in this school?... Japanese art knows this school more intimately than that of any people. In common use in their language there are many words like the word *edaburi*, which, translated as near as may be, means the formative arrangement of the branches of a tree. We have no such word in English, we are not yet sufficiently civilized to think in such terms, but the architect must not only learn to think in such terms but he must learn in this school to fashion his vocabulary for himself and furnish it in a comprehensive way with useful words as significant as this one."

——Frank Lloyd Wright, "In the Cause of Architecture,"
Architectural Record, 1908

キース・ヘリング

キース・ヘリング（1958～1990）は、アメリカの芸術家で、落書きとストリートアートを流行させました。日本への強い思い入れがあり、書道と水墨画を習い、日本に来て自分の個展を開く機会を得たときは喜びました。1980年代の同性愛やエイズ禍の問題に関する強力な社会運動家で政治活動家でした。彼自身もエイズと診断され、1990年に31歳で亡くなりました。

「ぼくにとって日本はいつも大きな存在だった——まるのままの東洋哲学や、もちろん書道もあるしね。それに、幼かったころ、おやじが海兵隊員で沖縄に配属されたんだ。おやじが仏像の前で撮ったスナップ写真が何枚もあるよ——だからいつも、日本のものにまるごと惹きつけられていたんだ。

日本に行きたくてたまらなかったから、東京のギャラリー・ワタリと1年間の独占契約をしたんだ。ジュアンとLA Ⅱを連れて行くことにした。そのころ、ぼくの仕事に対する注文は——まだとても安価で現金化できたので——ほとんどすべての展示会は現場で描いた——どんなギャラリーでも、その瞬間にその場でまるごと描いた。だから、東京に着いたら材料をすべて買って、ギャラリーで用意を

Keith Haring

Keith Haring (1958–1990), an American artist who brought graffiti and street art into the mainstream, had a special place in his heart for Japan. He studied Japanese calligraphy and sumi painting and was excited for the opportunity to travel and show his art in Japan. He was a powerful social and political activist on issues of homosexuality and the AIDS epidemic of the 1980s. Being diagnosed with AIDS himself, Haring died in 1990, at the age of 31.

"Japan has always meant a lot to me—the whole Eastern philosophy thing and, of course, the calligraphy. Also, when I was a little kid, my father, who was in the Marines, was stationed in Okinawa. There are snapshots of my father standing in front of Buddhas—so the whole Japanese idea has always fascinated me.

"Because of my anxiousness to go to Japan, I agree to a one-year exclusive contract with the Watari Gallery in Tokyo. I decide to take Juan as well as LA II. Now, at this time, because of the demand for my work—it was still very inexpensive and collectible—I approach almost all my shows by doing the work on site—painting the whole show in whatever gallery, right then and there.

整えて仕事を始めたんだ。

　東京でぼくらは奇妙な小集団だった……最初の晩、日本の昔ながらの旅館に泊った——床に敷いた畳の上で寝て、石の湯船に入った。だけど、ぼくらにはちょっと変な感じがした。次の日、都心に移動して東京ヒルトンにチェックインした。そこではLA Ⅱはまったく日本食を受け付けなかったので、チーズバーガーを食っていた。

　まもなくすると、ぼくは自分のすべての時間を割いて、ギャラリーの個展の作品作りに精を出していた。東京の人たちは、ぼくのことを知っていたよ。ちょうど落書きブームが始まっていて、ポップやヒップホップが知られ始めたところだったからね。ぼくら3人は——プエルトリコ人、黒人、白人の3人は——たちまちマスコミのスターになったんだ」

——キース・ヘリング、『公認伝記』、1992年

So, when we get to Tokyo, I buy all my materials. I set myself up in the gallery and begin to work.

"In Tokyo, we're this strange little group. . . . The first night in Tokyo, we stay in this very traditional hotel—sleeping on floor mats, bathing in stone bathtubs. But it's a little too weird for us. The next day, we move to the downtown district and check into the Tokyo Hilton, where LA II, who doesn't take to Japanese food at all, can get a cheeseburger.

"In the meantime, I spend almost all my time working on my show at the gallery. The people of Tokyo already know who I am; because the graffiti scene was just beginning they're just finding out about the Pop and Hip-Hop scenes. Almost immediately, the three of us—this Puerto Rican kid, this black kid, and this white kid—become media stars."

——Keith Haring, *Keith Haring: The Authorized Biography*, 1992

ヴィヴィアン・ウエストウッド

ヴィヴィアン・ウエストウッド（1941～）は、ロンドンを本拠に活躍するファッションデザイナーで、1970年代、パンクファッションを流行させて、世界のひのき舞台に上りました。世界中の多くの国々で自身のブランド店を開店し、日本にも店があります。

「私の人生最良の夜は、日本の能楽を観た夜ね。たった1回観ただけだけれど、今でもこう思うの。『こんな経験をまたできるのかしら？』ってね。とっても魅惑的で、複雑で、それに原始的だった。信じられないくらいだったわ」

—ヴィヴィアン・ウエストウッド、『ウォールストリート・ジャーナル』のインタビュー、2011年4月

Vivienne Westwood

Vivienne Westwood (1941–) is a London-based fashion designer who rose to the global stage by bringing punk fashion into the mainstream in the 1970s. She has opened stores devoted to carrying her label in many countries around the world, including Japan.

"The best night of my life was watching the Japanese Noh theater. I've only seen it once, but even saying it now, I think, 'How can I ever have this experience again?' It was so mesmerizing, so complicated and so primordial; I could not believe it."

——Vivienne Westwood, interview with the *Wall Street Journal*, April 2011

第5章
作家

Chapter 5
Writers

Walt Whitman
Oscar Wilde
William Butler Yeats
Ezra Pound
Jack Kerouac
David Mitchell

ウォルト・ホイットマン

ウォルト・ホイットマン（1819〜1892）は、アメリカの偉大な詩人の1人とみなされています。存命中、彼の詩は問題が多いと考えられていました。多くの人が、詩のなかに用いられている性的描写がみだらであると非難し、率直で制約にとらわれない書き方を批判した人もいました。この書き方は現在では「自由詩」と呼ばれています。ホイットマンはほぼ全生涯をニューヨーク州で過ごしました。1860年に日本初の外交使節団*がニューヨークに到着したとき、その訪問を記念して「The Errand-Bearers（使節団）」という詩を書きました。ここにその第1節を紹介します。

海を越えて遥か日本から渡来した、
礼儀正しい、アジアの、日に焼けた頬をした貴公子たち、
先着者、客人、2本の刀を差した貴公子たち、
知恵を授ける貴公子たち、無蓋の馬車に身をゆだね、
無帽のまま平然として、
今日、マンハッタンの街頭を行く。

——ウォルト・ホイットマン「The Errand-Bearers（使節団）」後に
「ブロードウェーの華麗な行列」と改題、1860年

＊1860年、開国後初となるアメリカへの公式訪問団のこと。護衛についた咸臨丸には、勝海舟、福沢諭吉が乗船した。

Walt Whitman

Walt Whitman (1819–1892) is considered one of America's greatest poets. His poetry was considered controversial during his lifetime: many accused him of obscenity for using sexual imagery in his poetry, while others criticized his open, unrestrained way of writing, which we call "free verse" today. Whitman lived in New York State for almost his entire life. In 1860, the first Japanese diplomatic mission to New York arrived, and Whitman wrote a poem called "The Errand-Bearers" to commemorate their visit. Here is the first stanza of that poem:

Over sea, hither from Niphon,
Courteous, the Princes of Asia, swart-cheek'd princes,
First-comers, guests, two-sworded princes,
Lesson-giving princes, leaning back in their open barouches, bare-headed, impassive,
This day they ride through Manhattan.

——Walt Whitman, "The Errand-Bearers," also known as "A Broadway Pageant," 1860

オスカー・ワイルド

オスカー・ワイルド（1854〜1900）は、アイルランド出身の作家、批評家、劇作家で、同時代の多くの芸術家と同じく、日本の芸術と文化の賞賛者でした。ワイルドは才気あふれる作家であり理論家でした。1882年、講演旅行でアメリカ全土を周りました。そのときの「イギリスの芸術復興」という講演のなかで、日本の芸術が当時の西洋の芸術形式とどのように異なり、どのような影響を与えたか述べています。

「そして、これこそ（芸術が感覚に訴える要素を受け入れたこと）がまさに、東洋の芸術がヨーロッパの我々におよぼしつつある影響の、またあらゆる日本画の魅力の理由なのです。西洋世界がその世界独自の知的懐疑と独自の悲哀の精神的悲劇という耐えきれぬ重荷を芸術に負わせてきたのに対し、東洋は芸術本来の絵画的条件に常に忠実でありました」

——オスカー・ワイルド「イギリスの芸術復興」、1882年

Oscar Wilde

Oscar Wilde (1854–1900), an Irish writer, journalist, and playwright, was an admirer of Japanese art and culture, along with many of his contemporaries. Wilde was a brilliant writer and theorist, and in 1882, he traveled throughout the U.S. on a lecture tour. His lecture, "The English Renaissance of Art," mentions how Japanese art differed from and influenced Western art forms at the time.

"And this indeed is the reason of the influence which Eastern art is having on us in Europe, and of the fascination of all Japanese work. While the Western world has been laying on art the intolerable burden of its own intellectual doubts and the spiritual tragedy of its own sorrows, the East has always kept true to art's primary and pictorial conditions."

——Oscar Wilde, "The English Renaissance of Art," 1882

ウィリアム・バトラー・イエーツ

西洋の多くの人は、ウィリアム・バトラー・イエーツ（1865〜1939）を20世紀の最も偉大な詩人の1人とみなしています。彼は出身地のアイルランドの遺産を誇りにし、自作の詩にたびたびアイルランドの英雄や人物を登場させています。当時の西洋の芸術家や作家の多くと同様に、日本の芸術を高く評価していました。以下の一節は、日本の作家で詩人である友人の野口米次郎*に宛てた手紙の抜粋です。ここでイエーツは自分の作品にどのように日本の美学を取り入れようとしたか説明しています。

「……あなたの国の広重は、ぼくを大いに喜ばせてくれました。ぼくは東洋の芸術からますます喜びを感じ、自分が作品にめざしているものと東洋の芸術が同じだということを強く意識するようになりました。この200年から300年のヨーロッパの絵画は、ぼくが年を重ねるにつれ、よそよそしく見え、まるで外国語で語りかけられている気がします……あなたの国の画家はみな簡素で、スコットランドのバラッドかアイルランドの物語の創案者のようです……ぼく自身も簡素な人間になりたかったのですが、その方法がわかりません。年を取ればその方法が見つかるかもしれないと願いつつ、あなたが送ってくださったような書

William Butler Yeats

Many people in the West consider William Butler Yeats (1865–1939) one of the greatest poets of the 20th century. He was proud of his Irish heritage and often featured Irish heroes and figures in his poetry. He greatly admired Japanese art, as many Western artists and writers at the time did. In the passage below, which is an excerpt from a letter he wrote to his friend Yonejiro Noguchi, a Japanese writer and poet, Yeats explains how he tries to incorporate Japanese aesthetics into his own work.

". . . your Hiroshige has given me the greatest pleasure. I take more and more pleasure from oriental art, find more and more that it accords with what I aim at in my own work. European painting of the last two or three hundred years grows strange to me as I grow older, begins to speak as with a foreign tongue . . . all of your painters are simple, like the writers of Scottish ballads or the inventors of Irish stories . . . I would be simple myself but I do not know how. I am always turning over pages like those you have sent me hoping that in my old age I may discover how. I wish some Japanese would

物をいつもめくっています。これらの画家たちの生活すべて——彼らの会話、愛、信仰、友人——について、誰か日本の人が語ってくれないかと願っています。このようなことを詳しく知りたい、そして彼らがどんな家に住んでいたか知りたいのです。まだ建っているとしたらですが……そうすれば、彼らがどれほど簡素に生きていたか理解しやすくなるかもしれません。ヨーロッパでは美の形は1世代も続きませんが、日本では何世紀も続いているのですね」

——ウィリアム・バトラー・イエーツ、野口米次郎への手紙、1921年

＊野口米次郎：1875-1947　渡米後、詩人、作家として活躍。彫刻家のイサム＝ノグチの父。

tell us all about the lives—their talks, their loves, their religions, their friends—of these painters. I would like to know these things minutely, and to know what their houses looked like, if they still stand . . . It might make it more easy to understand their simplicity. A form of beauty scarcely lasts a generation with us, but with you it lasts for centuries."

——William Butler Yeats, letter to Yonejiro Noguchi, 1921

エズラ・パウンド

エズラ・パウンド（1885～1972）は、アメリカから国外に移住して暮らした詩人、作家、政治活動家で、文学のモダニズム運動の形成に一役買いました。日本の芸術、詩、演劇、言語に感動し、魅了され、日本の地を踏んだことはありませんが、第二次世界大戦の間、しばらく『ジャパン・タイムズ』のコラムニストを務めました。パウンドは才能豊かな詩人でしたが、アメリカ合衆国に反逆罪で起訴され、ワシントンD.C.の精神病院に送られ、そこで12年間過ごしました。日本に造詣の深い学者、アーネスト・フェノロサと共作した、能や謡曲を翻訳して説明した作品は、英訳された日本文学のリストのなかで古典として残っています。

「能が世界で最も偉大な芸術の1つであることに疑問の余地はなく、おそらく、最も難解な芸術の1つといえるだろう」

——エズラ・パウンド、『日本の古典能楽』の「序章」から、1959年

「私のような人間なら、『葵の上』のようなトーキー映画を数本もらえば、喜んでグアムを差し出すでしょう」

——エズラ・パウンド、ローマ日本大使への手紙、児玉実英編『Ezra Pound and Japan: Letters and Essays（エズラ・パウンドと日本：書簡と随筆）』に転載、1987年

Ezra Pound

Ezra Pound (1885–1972) was an American expatriate poet, writer, and political activist who helped form the modernist movement in literature. He was inspired and fascinated by Japanese art, poetry, theater, and language, and although he never set foot in Japan, he was a columnist for the *Japan Times* for a short time during World War II. Although Pound was a brilliant poet, he was arrested for treason by the U.S. and spent 12 years in a mental institution in Washington, D.C. His work with Ernest Fenollosa, a scholar on Japan, on translating and interpreting Noh plays and poetry, live on as classics in the canon of translated Japanese literature in English.

"The Noh is unquestionably one of the great arts of the world, and it is possibly one of the most recondite."

——Ezra Pound, *The Classic Noh Theatre of Japan*, "Introduction, "1959

"Men like myself would cheerfully give you Guam for a few sound films such as that of *Awoi no Uye*."

——Ezra Pound, letter to the Japanese ambassador to Rome, reprinted in *Ezra Pound and Japan: Letters and Essays*, edited by Sanehide Kodama, 1987

ジャック・ケルアック

ジャック・ケルアック（1922～1969）は、アメリカの最も有名な小説家および詩人の1人で、「ビート族」文化運動の創始者の1人として知られています。「意識の流れ」のような一種の現代の文体を提唱したと考えられています。一時、禅宗と日本哲学を学びました。

「ぼくの作品に実際に影響を与えたのは大乗仏教です。これは釈迦牟尼、つまり釈迦本人による原始仏教で、昔のインドで……。禅は釈迦が残されたもの、あるいは菩提（ぼだい）で、中国を経て日本に広まりました。ぼくの文体に影響を与えた禅は、俳句のなかに見られます。さっきも言ったように、俳句というのは17音節でできた3行詩で、芭蕉、一茶、子規などによって数百年前に書かれ、現在にも名人がいます。文中で思考が突然飛躍する短くて快い文は、俳句の一種と言えます。それはとても自由で、作者自身を驚かせる面白みがあるのです。木の枝から小鳥に、おもむくままに心を飛躍させてみようじゃありませんか」

――ジャック・ケルアック、『パリス・レビュー』誌のインタビュー、1968年

Jack Kerouac

Jack Kerouac (1922–1969), one of America's most famous novelists and poets, is known as one of the godfathers of the "Beat" cultural movement. He is thought to have pioneered some contemporary forms of writing, such as "stream of consciousness." For a time, he studied Zen Buddhism and Japanese philosophy.

"What's really influenced my work is the Mahayana Buddhism, the original Buddhism of Gautama Sàkyamuni, the Buddha himself, of the India of old . . . Zen is what's left of his Buddhism, or Bodhi, after its passing into China and then into Japan. The part of Zen that's influenced my writing is the Zen contained in the haiku, like I said, the three-line, seventeen-syllable poems written hundreds of years ago by guys like Basho, Issa, Shiki, and there've been recent masters. A sentence that's short and sweet with a sudden jump of thought in it is a kind of haiku, and there's a lot of freedom and fun in surprising yourself with that, let the mind willy-nilly jump from the branch to the bird."

——Jack Kerouac, *Paris Review* interview, 1968

デイヴィッド・ミッチェル

デイヴィッド・ミッチェル（1969〜）は、イギリスの小説家で、8年間、広島で暮らし、教鞭を取りました。彼の小説の多くは、登場人物が日本人で日本が舞台になっているか、あるいは彼の日本像が描かれています。ミッチェルの最も有名な小説は、『クラウド・アトラス』でしょう。この作品は叙事詩的な映画になり、3人の監督がメガホンをとりました。2007年、ミッチェルは『タイム』誌の「世界で最も影響力のある100人」の1人に選ばれました。彼の作品には日本文化が多大な影響を与えています。ここに、彼が日本文化から受けた影響について述べた随筆の抜粋を紹介します。

「西洋での日本のイメージは決まりきっていて、ぼくはそれに賛成できません。日本は桜、芸者、富士山、特攻隊員の国と見られているのです。ぼくは村上春樹のように日本をありのままに描き、醜悪のなかに美を見つけたいのです。そのためには、日本人を主人公にするのがより説得力のある方法のように思えます」

——デイヴィッド・ミッチェル、Beatrice.com でのインタビュー、2001年

David Mitchell

David Mitchell (1969–) is an English novelist who spent eight years living and teaching in Hiroshima. Many of his novels feature Japanese characters and settings or capture his vision of Japan. Mitchell is perhaps most famous for his novel *Cloud Atlas*, which was made into an epic motion picture directed by three different directors. In 2007, *Time* magazine listed Mitchell as one of the 100 most influential people in the world. Japanese culture has had a profound effect on David Mitchell's writing. This is an excerpt from an essay he wrote about how Japanese culture has influenced him:

"I have a problem with the way Japan is usually portrayed in the West, as the land of cherry blossoms, geishas, Mt. Fuji, and kamikaze pilots. I wanted to do what Haruki Murakami does, depicting Japan as it is, and finding the beauty in the ugliness. Using Japanese protagonists seems to be a more convincing way to go about that."

——David Mitchell, interview with *Beatrice.com*, 2001

第6章
音楽家

Chapter 6
Musicians

Miles Davis
John Lennon
Michael Jackson
Beyoncé Knowles
Lady Gaga
Gwen Stefani
Yo-Yo Ma

マイルス・デイビス

マイルス・デイビス（1926～1991）は、世界一流のジャズ演奏家およびトランペット奏者の1人です。ビーバップ、クールジャズ、フュージョンなど多くのタイプのジャズに影響を与えました。熱烈なファン層がいる日本では、1964年に初めて演奏しました。この初コンサートは『マイルス・イン・トーキョー』というライブアルバムになりました。その後、何度も来日し、日本と日本国民をますます賞賛し尊敬するようになりました。

「ぼくにとって世界で最も素敵な女性は、ブラジル、エチオピア、それに日本の女性たちだ。素敵というのは、美しさ、女らしさ、知性、振る舞い、身のこなし、そして男性に対する敬意をすべて兼ね備えているということだ。日本、エチオピア、ブラジルの女性は男性を尊敬し、けっして男のように振る舞わない――少なくとも、ぼくの知っている女性たちはね」

——マイルス・デイビス、『マイルス・デイビス自叙伝』、1989年

Miles Davis

Miles Davis (1926–1991) was one of the world's foremost jazz musicians and trumpeters. He had an influence on many types of jazz, including bebop, cool jazz, and jazz fusion. Davis had a huge fan base in Japan, where he played for the first time in 1964. This first concert was turned into a live album called *Miles in Tokyo*, and he was to return many more times to Japan, developing an admiration and respect for the country and the people.

"The finest women in the world for me are Brazilian, Ethiopian, and Japanese women. And here I mean a combination of beauty, femininity, intelligence, the way they carry themselves, their body carriage, and the respect they have for a man. Japanese, Ethiopian, and Brazilian women respect men and don't ever try acting like a man—at least the ones I've known."

——Miles Davis, *Miles, the Autobiography*, 1989

「ぼくたちは東京に行って、そこで数回コンサートをした。ぼくにとって初めての日本の旅だった。フランシスも同行して、日本食や日本文化すべてを学んだ。そのころには、ベン・シャピロという巡業公演マネージャーがいて、ぼくから事務的な仕事の重荷を下してくれた。バンドに支払ったり、ホテルや航空券を取ったり、そんなこまごましたことをね。それで自由な時間ができた。ぼくたちは東京と大阪で公演した。日本に着いたときのことはけっして忘れないよ。日本への飛行はくそ長いので、コカインと睡眠薬を持ち込み、両方とも飲んだ。それでも眠れなかったので、酒も飲んだ。着陸すると、大勢の人たちが空港で出迎えてくれた。飛行機を降りると、みんなが言うんだ。『ようこそ、日本へ、マイルス・デイビス』って。そのあとぼくは、そこらじゅうに吐きまくったんだ。でも、だれもとまどったりしなかった。薬物治療をして麻薬を抜いてくれ、まるで王様のように扱ってくれた。ああ、ほんとうに楽しかった。それ以来、日本人を尊敬し、好きになった。素晴らしい人たちだ。いつも大歓迎してくれる。もちろんコンサートは大成功だったよ」

——マイルス・デイビス、『マイルス・デイビス自叙伝』、1989年

"We traveled to Tokyo to play some concerts over there. It was my first trip to Japan, and Frances went along and learned all about Japanese food and culture. By this time I had a road manager named Ben Shapiro, so he took a lot of business off my shoulders, like paying the band, getting hotels and flights, and shit like that. That left me free to enjoy myself. We played Tokyo and Osaka. I'll never forget my arrival in Japan. Flying to Japan is a long-ass flight. So I brought coke and sleeping pills with me and I took both. Then I couldn't go to sleep so I was drinking, too. When we landed there were all these people to meet us at the airport. We're getting off the plane and they're saying, 'Welcome to Japan, Miles Davis,' and I threw up all over everything. But they didn't miss a beat. They got me some medicine and got me straight and treated me like a king. Man, I had a ball, and I have respected and loved the Japanese people ever since. Beautiful people. They have always treated me great. The concerts were a big success."

——Miles Davis, *Miles, the Autobiography*, 1989

ジョン・レノン

ジョン・レノン (1940〜1980)は、おそらく世界で最も有名な現代音楽家の1人で、平和活動家でもありました。イギリスの人気バンド「ビートルズ」の共同創設者として世界的な名声を得ました。しかし、わずか40歳でニューヨークにおいて暗殺されるという悲劇的な最期を迎えました。妻は日本人芸術家のオノ・ヨーコです。

ヨーコの芸術について

「ヨーコはぼくにとって、ポールとディランを合わせて1つにしたような重要な存在だ。彼女が生きている間に認められるとは思っていない。彼女を認めている人間としては、まずぼくがいるし、彼女が何者で、何を思っているか、このばかばかしい世代にとって彼女の芸術が何を意味するのか少しでも理解できる人間は、片手で数えられるぐらいはいるだろう。彼女は、いずれ認められるかもしれないという希望を持っている。もし、ぼくが認められなければ、ぼくはピエロの衣装に身を包んでやっているか、街頭でやっているか、えーと、その他何かしらをやっているよ——とにかく、ぼくはヨーコの芸術を評価しているんだ」

——ジョン・レノン、『ローリング・ストーン』誌のインタビュー、1971年

John Lennon

John Lennon (1940–1980) was perhaps one of the world's most famous contemporary musicians as well as a peace activist. He rose to global fame as a co-founder of the British megaband The Beatles, but his life came to a tragic end when he was assassinated in New York when he was only 40 years old. He was married to Yoko Ono, a Japanese artist.

On Yoko's art:

"Yoko is as important to me as Paul and Dylan rolled into one. I don't think she will get recognition until she's dead. There's me, and maybe I could count the people on one hand that have any conception of what she is or what her mind is like, or what her work means to this fuckin' idiotic generation. She has the hope that she might be recognized. If I can't get recognized, and I'm doing it in a fuckin' clown's costume, I'm doing it on the streets, you know, I don't know what—I admire Yoko's work."

——John Lennon, interview with *Rolling Stone*, 1971

ヨーコに関する世評について

「彼女はぼくと出会うまでは順調だった。ハワード・スミスがFMラジオで彼女の音楽をかけると発表したら、ばかどもが電話をかけてきたんだ。『そんなもの絶対にかけるな。彼女はビートルズを解散せたんだぞ』ってね。彼女がビートルズを解散させたわけではないし、たとえそうであったとしても、それがFMラジオのことや彼女のレコードと何の関係があるというんだ？　彼女は女性で、おまけに日本人だ。彼女に対して人種的偏見があるし、女だからという偏見もある。そういうことなんだ」

——ジョン・レノン、『ローリング・ストーン』誌のオリジナルインタビュー、1971年；テキストは2000年の改訂版より

On public opinion about Yoko:

"She was doing all right before she met me. Howard Smith announced he was going to play her music on FM and all these idiots rang up and said, "Don't you dare play it, she split the Beatles." She didn't split the Beatles and even if she did what does that have to do with it or her fucking record? She is a woman, and she's Japanese; there is racial prejudice against her and there is female prejudice against her. It's as simple as that."

——John Lennon, original interview with *Rolling Stone*, 1971; text revised by *Rolling Stone* in 2000

マイケル・ジャクソン

マイケル・ジャクソン（1958〜2009）は、世界中に「キング・オブ・ポップ」として知られたアメリカのシンガー・ソングライターで、全キャリアを通してポップ・ミュージックに多大な影響を与えました。彼のキャリアは1960年代の家族バンド、ジャクソン5のリードボーカルから2000年代に突然亡くなるまで続きました。

——今回で日本への訪問は5回目です。滞在中、特にやりたいと思われていることはありますか？

「ファンは忠誠心が厚くて、ぼくをとても愛してくれる。ぼくも彼らを愛しているよ。なにしろ30年間も熱心に応援してくれているんだ。とても忠実で愛すべき……」

——日本で最初の（ソロ）ツアーは1987年のBad（バッド）ツアーでした。日本は何か変わったと思われますか？

「日本が？　ぼくはいつも技術に注目している。次に何が出てくるか、いつも興味を持っている。今はデジタル化に夢中になっているようで——物が小型になり、性能が良く、えー、鮮明になっている。それに、子どもたちだ。わかるだろ、小さな丸顔のね。それに赤ちゃん……みんな大好きだよ」

　——マイケル・ジャクソン、NTB（日本テレビ）のインタビュー、1996年

Michael Jackson

Michael Jackson (1958–2009), known worldwide as the "King of Pop," was an American singer and songwriter who had a tremendous influence on pop music throughout his entire career, which spanned from the 1960s as the lead singer of his family band, Jackson 5, to his sudden death in the 2000s.

—It's going to be your fifth visit in Japan. Are there any things you are especially looking forward to doing during your stay?

"I think the loyalty of the fans and the love is very high too. I love them and they've been great for thirty years. Very loyal and loving..."

—Your first (solo) tour in Japan was the Bad tour in 1987. Do you find any changes in Japan?

"In Japan? I always notice the technology. I'm always interested in what you're going to do next. It's like there is a digital craze going on now—make it smaller and it becomes bigger you know, clearer. And the children, you know with their little round faces and the babies... I love them."

———Michael Jackson, interview with NTV, 1996

ビヨンセ・ノウルズ

ビヨンセ・ノウルズ（1981〜）は、少女たちのポップ・トリオ、デスティニーズ・チャイルドのリードボーカルとして世界中で脚光を浴びました。2003年にソロ活動を始めてからも、世界で爆発的な人気を得ています。力強い振り付けと、精力的なライブ・パフォーマンスを観て、ビヨンセを世界最高のエンターテーナーの1人と呼ぶ音楽批評家もいます。最近は、自身の世界的な知名度を利用して、フェミニズムと女性の権利拡大のメッセージを唱えています。

「日本滞在中、デスティニーズ・チャイルドが『インディペンデント・ウーマン』を発表したときのことを覚えているわ。日本の女性たちは、仕事、独立した考え、目標を持っていることがいかに誇らしいか語ってくれた。それを聞いて、とてもうれしかった。そして、私の責任の1つは、女性たちをもっとしっかりと励ますことだと気づいたの」

——ビヨンセ・ノウルズ、『クレイジー・イン・ラブ：ビヨンセ・ノウルズ自伝』、2011年

Beyoncé Knowles

Beyoncé Knowles (1981–) became an international sensation as the lead singer of girl-group pop-trio Destiny's Child. She continued to take the world by storm when she launched her solo career in 2003. With her powerful choreography and high-octane live performances, Beyoncé has been called one of the best entertainers in the world by some music critics. In recent years, she has also used her high international profile to advance messages of feminism and women's empowerment.

"I remember being in Japan when Destiny's Child put out 'Independent Women,' and women there were saying how proud they were to have their own jobs, their own independent thinking, their own goals. It made me feel so good, and I realized that one of my responsibilities was to inspire women in a deeper way."

―Beyoncé Knowles, *Crazy In Love: The Beyoncé Knowles Biography*, 2011

レディー・ガガ

レディー・ガガ（1986〜）は、アメリカのシンガー・ソングライターおよびパフォーマーで、2008年にデビューアルバム『ザ・フェイム』を掲げて世界的にポップ・ミュージック界に登場しました。それ以後も、独自の芸術的な歌の解釈と女性の権利拡大のメッセージを通して、音楽業界に貢献し、影響を与え続けています。

「あらゆる種類の音楽を聴いたけれど、J-ポップが大好きよ。それに、その自由さが気に入っているの。J-ポップのエネルギーはすごく強烈で、音楽活動をしているとき、いつも日本文化から着想を得ているわ。それにアルバムを作っていたときも、日本文化からとても着想を得たわ。こんなのはどうかしら、日本文化にドイツの前衛的な芸術文化、フランスのダンス音楽、シカゴのテクノ音楽とヒップホップを混ぜるのよ——そんなことをやりたいと思っていたの」

——レディー・ガガ、アルバム『アートポップ』日本盤に録音されたインタビュー、2013年

Lady Gaga

Lady Gaga (1986–) is an American singer, songwriter and performer. She broke onto the international pop music scene in 2008 with her debut album, *The Fame*. She has continued to contribute to and influence the music industry with her artistic interpretations of songs and messages of women's empowerment.

"I listen to all different kinds of music and I love J-pop. And I love the freedom of the music. The energy in J-pop is really powerful, and I'm always inspired by Japanese culture when working and I was very inspired by Japanese culture when I was making the album. I would say Japanese culture mixed with German underground art culture and French dance music and Chicago techno and hip hop—these were the things that I was thinking about."

——Lady Gaga, interview recorded for the Japanese edition of her album
ARTPOP, 2013

グウェン・ステファニー

グウェン・ステファニー（1965～）は、アメリカの歌手、俳優、ファッションデザイナーで、1990年代の人気ロックバンド、ノー・ダウトのリードボーカルとして有名になりました。ソロ歌手として世界中で何百万枚ものアルバムを売って大成功したのち、洋服ブランドを立ち上げました。彼女によると、日本文化に影響を受けたブランドだということです。次に4人の日本人バックダンサーを雇い、「原宿ガールズ」と命名しました。彼女たちはステファニーと踊るだけでなく、付き人として働きました。このことでマスコミと世間から批判を浴びることになりました。原宿ガールズを小道具や操り人形として使うのは潜在的な人種差別だと言うのです。

「私にとって原宿ガールズとの仕事は、彼女たちに対する純粋な賛辞とファン精神から来ているの。誰かのファンになってはいけないと言うの？　それともほかの文化のファンに？　もちろん、かまわないわよね。もちろん、ほかの文化をほめたっていいのよ。これは日本文化とアメリカ文化の間で起こったことなの。（「原宿ガールズ」の）歌詞にあるように、ピンポンゲームなのよ。私たちがアメリカっぽいことをすると、日本人はそれを取り入れ、手を加え、とても日本的でかっこのいいものにする。今度は、私

Gwen Stefani

Gwen Stefani (1965–) is an American singer, actor, and fashion designer who rose to fame as the lead vocalist of No Doubt, a popular 1990s rock band. After launching a successful solo career that sold millions of albums worldwide, she created a clothing line that she said was influenced by Japanese culture. She went on to hire four Japanese back-up dancers, who she dubbed the "Harajuku Girls." They not only performed with her but also acted as her entourage. This drew criticism from both the media and the public, who felt that her use of the Harajuku Girls as props or puppets was latently racist.

"For me, everything that I did with the Harajuku Girls was just a pure compliment and being a fan. You can't be a fan of somebody else? Or another culture? Of course you can. Of course you can celebrate other cultures. That's what Japanese culture and American culture have done. It's like I say in the song ["Harajuku Girls"]: it's a ping-pong match. We do something American, they take it and they flip it and make it so Japanese and so cool. And we take it back and go, 'Whoa, that's so

たちがそれを取り戻して言うの。『すごい、なんてかっこいいんだ！』ってね。本当に素晴らしいのよ。世界的にも素晴らしいものになっていて、これこそ２つの文化が融合した結果なのよ。私には何か悪いことをしたという気持ちはなく、ただこの愛を分かち合っただけなのよ。そうしたければ、否定的な見方をしてもいいけれど、私に対する疑念は取り除いてほしいわ。だって、まじめな話、すべては愛から生まれているのよ」

　　――グウェン・ステファニー、『タイム』誌のインタビュー、2014年

cool!' That's so beautiful. It's a beautiful thing in the world, how our cultures come together. I don't feel like I did anything but share that love. You can look at it from a negative point of view if you want to, but get off my cloud. Because, seriously, that was all meant out of love."

——Gwen Stefani, interview with *TIME*, 2014

ヨーヨー・マ

ヨーヨー・マ（1955～）は、おそらく世界で最も有名なチェロ奏者です。中国系アメリカ人で、パリで生まれ、ニューヨーク市で育ちました。幼いころから音楽の神童として知られ、初めて観衆の前で演奏したのは5歳のときでした。7歳のとき、アメリカ大統領、ドワイト・D・アイゼンハワーとジョン・F・ケネディの前で演奏しました。90枚以上のアルバムを発表し、多くの音楽賞を受賞しています。

「日本に行くのは楽しいです。日本という国が教えてくれるのは、国が結束し、犯罪の恐怖に——それが現実のものであっても想像上のものであっても——圧倒されなければ、社会が何を成し遂げられるかということです。たくさんのものをあきらめなければならないけれど、たくさんのものが得られます。だから文化の違う国を訪れることは大事なのです——暮らしの可能性について、新しいアイディアを見つけることができるからです」

——ヨーヨー・マ、『ボルチモア・サン』紙のインタビュー、1994年

Yo-Yo Ma

Yo-Yo Ma (1955–) is perhaps the world's best-known cello player. A Chinese American who was born in Paris, Yo-Yo Ma was raised in New York City. He was considered a musical prodigy from a very young age, and began performing publicly when he was five years old. He performed for U.S. presidents Dwight D. Eisenhower and John F. Kennedy when he was seven years old. He has released more than 90 albums and received numerous musical awards.

"I love coming to Japan. It shows you what a society can accomplish when it's united and when it's not consumed by the fear of crime, whether real or imagined. You give up a lot, but you get a lot too. That's why traveling to other cultures is important—it gives you fresh ideas about the possibilities for living."

—— Yo Yo Ma, interview with the *Baltimore Sun*, 1994

第7章
俳優と映画製作者

Chapter 7
Actors and Movie Makers

Steven Spielberg
Quentin Tarantino
Roman Coppola
Roger Ebert
Bill Murray
Clint Eastwood
Tommy Lee Jones
Hugh Grant
Tom Cruise
Edward Norton

スティーヴン・スピルバーグ

スティーヴン・スピルバーグ（1946〜）は、アメリカの映画監督で、現代の大ヒット映画の概念を作ったことで知られています。アカデミー監督賞を2度受賞し、40年以上にわたる経歴を通して、ハリウッドに大きな影響を与えてきました。彼が英雄とみなす人の1人は、日本の映画監督、黒澤明です。

「黒澤監督が、あの年齢で——たしか70代です——あんなに生き生きと、あんなに才能豊かに、あんなに精力的に自分の流儀で映画を作り映画に魔法をかけておられるのを見ると、ぼくらの世代にとって良い前兆であってほしいと願うばかりです。黒澤監督の爪の垢を煎じて飲めるなら、そしてぼくらの世代が70代や80代まで映画を作れるなら、将来に希望が持てます。とても楽しみにしています」

——スティーヴン・スピルバーグ、日本のテレビのインタビュー、1982年

Steven Spielberg

Steven Spielberg (1946–) is an American movie director who is considered to have conceptualized the modern "blockbuster" movie. Spielberg has won two Academy Awards for Best Director and has been highly influential in Hollywood during his career that has spanned more than four decades. One of his heroes is Japanese movie director Akira Kurosawa.

"If Mr. Kurosawa can be so vital and so talented and so energetic about his movie making and his movie magic at his age—he's in his seventies—I can only hope that that bodes well for my generation. If we could take a lesson from Mr. Kurosawa, if my generation could make movies into our seventies and eighties, that's a happy thought for the future. It's something to look forward to."

———Steven Spielberg, interview with Japanese TV, 1982

クエンティン・タランチーノ

クエンティン・タランチーノ（1963〜）は、アメリカの映画監督で、1990年代に『パルプ・フィクション』が封切られて世界的な名声を得ました。存命中の最も影響力のある映画監督の1人として知られ、しばしば日本の映画、アニメーション、漫画をインスピレーションの源として評価しています。

「個人的には、今、ぼくの好きな映画は日本で製作されているこういった暴力的な大衆映画です。お気に入りの監督グループに関する限りは……大好きなアメリカの監督もたくさんいますが……グループとして好みなのは、日本でそういう種類の映画を撮っているすべての監督たちです。お察しの通り、三池崇史、石井隆、石井聰亙たちのことを言っているのです」

——クエンティン・タランチーノ、『映画秘宝』誌のインタビュー、
2003年8月28日

Quentin Tarantino

American director Quentin Tarantino (1963–) rose to worldwide fame in the 1990s with the release of *Pulp Fiction*. Tarantino is considered one of the most influential movie directors alive today, and he often credits Japanese films, animation, and manga as sources of inspiration.

"Personally, my favorite cinema right now is this violent pop cinema coming out of Japan. As far as a group of directors that are my favorites . . . and there's a lot of American directors that I really like . . . my favorite as far as a group is all the directors doing those kinds of movies in Japan. Obviously, I'm talking about Takashi Miike, Takashi Ishii, Sogo Ishii."

——Quentin Tarantino, interview with *Eiga HIHO* magazine,
August 28, 2003

ロマン・コッポラ

ロマン・コッポラ（1965〜）は、有名な映画監督、フランシス・フォード・コッポラの息子で、才能のある映画監督で生まれながらのビジョナリー（先見の明のある人）です。やはり映画監督である妹のソフィア・コッポラと多くのプロジェクトで一緒に仕事をすることがしばしばあります。2012年の映画『ムーンライズ・キングダム』では、アカデミー脚本賞の候補に挙がりました。

「ぼくが最も夢中になっている国は日本です。京都には俵屋旅館というのがあって、それが並外れて素晴らしいんです。ぼくは日本文化に魅せられています。食べ物、衣服、作法、伝統にね。一番感動したのは日本を旅した経験です。

——ロマン・コッポラ、『インデペンデント』紙のインタビュー、
2012年12月14日

Roman Coppola

Roman Coppola (1965–) is the son of famed movie director Francis Ford Coppola and is a talented movie director and visionary in his own right. He often works with his sister Sophia Coppola, also a director, on many projects. He was an Oscar nominee for Best Original Screenplay for the 2012 movie, *Moonrise Kingdom*.

"Japan is the most intoxicating place for me. In Kyoto, there's an inn called the Tawaraya which is quite extraordinary. The Japanese culture fascinates me: the food, the dress, the manners and the traditions. It's the travel experience that has moved me the most."

——Roman Coppola, interview with *The Independent*, December 14, 2012

ロジャー・イーバート

ロジャー・イーバート（1942〜2013）は、ジャーナリストで映画評論家です。40年以上にわたり、アメリカの聴衆に映画を理解し鑑賞する力をつけることに貢献してきました。アメリカで最も有名な映画評論家で、しばしば外国映画の批評を書き、多くのアメリカ人に初めて外国映画の手ほどきをしました。最も好きな映画監督の1人が宮崎駿で、1999年に『シカゴ・サンタイムズ』紙のレビューで宮崎監督について書いています。

「大半の映画インタビューは、ジャーナリストにとって単なる仕事か作業であるが、時には天才に出会うことがある。そんなとき私は、黙って、心を集中し、すべてを覚えておこうとする。例えば、ベルイマン、ヒッチコック、フェリーニにインタビューしたときだった。9月に再びそんな経験をした。それはトロントで宮崎駿にインタビューしたときだ。

宮崎駿という名前になじみがないかもしれない。たとえ映画好きの人でも、彼の映画を気に入るかどうか、まだわからないのだから。彼とスタジオジブリの共同制作者である高畑勲（『火垂るの墓』）は、アニメーション映画において世界で最も偉大な監督と言えるだろう」

——ロジャー・イーバート、「宮崎監督、アメリカの注意を惹く」、
『シカゴ・サンタイムズ』、1999年

Roger Ebert

Journalist and movie critic Roger Ebert (1942–2013) helped shape American audiences' understanding of and appreciation for movies for over forty years. He was America's best-known movie critic, and he often reviewed foreign films, introducing many Americans to foreign movies for the first time. One of his favorite directors was Hayao Miyazaki, whom he wrote about in a review for the *Chicago Sun-Times* in 1999.

"Most movie interviews are a job or work for the journalist, but sometimes you find yourself in the presence of a genius, and then you grow still and attentive, trying to remember everything. So it was when I interviewed Bergman, Hitchcock and Fellini, and so it was again in September, when I interviewed Hayao Miyazaki in Toronto.

"The name is unfamiliar to you because, while you love movies, you have not yet discovered that you would love his movies. He and his Studio Ghibli collaborator Isao Takahata (Grave of the Fireflies) are arguably the greatest directors of animation in the world."

——Roger Ebert, "Director Miyazaki Draws American Attention," *Chicago Sun-Times*, 1999

ビル・マーレイ

ビル・マーレイ（1950～）は、アメリカの俳優で、『ゴーストバスターズ』、『恋はデジャブ』、『ボールズ・ボールズ』などの映画で有名で、喜劇的な役割を多く演じています。しかし、2003年の映画『ロスト・イン・トランスレーション』では、東洋と西洋の間の文化の違いから生じる混乱を乗り超える、年老いてくたびれた俳優役で主演しました。インタビューで、実生活で日本に滞在したときの感想を述べています。

——日本では、少しでも"ロスト・イン・トランスレーション（言葉が通じずに困ること）"の体験をされましたか？

「福岡で友人と10日間過ごして、そこでゴルフトーナメントに出場しました。とても楽しく過ごしました。福岡では（東京から来た人たち）をからかうのです。まるで南部にいるみたいでした。彼らはまるでアメリカ人がニューヨーク市民をからかうみたいに、東京の人たちをからかっていました。東京の人たちはみな、すごく緊張してピリピリしていましたよ。あそこにいるのは、いつも楽しかった。誰も私の話す言葉を理解できないところにいるのは、面白かったです。誰にも知られていないところにいるのも愉快でした。そうすると、まったく自由に振る舞えますし、抑えられない邪悪な衝動を気兼ねなく実行できますからね。私にはそれが"ロスト・イン・トランスレーション"なのか、そうでないのかはわかりませんがね」

——ビル・マーレイ、アバウト・コムのインタビュー、2003年

Bill Murray

Bill Murray (1950–), an American actor famed for his role in such movies as *Ghostbusters*, *Groundhog Day*, and *Caddyshack*, is often cast in comedic roles. However, in the 2003 film *Lost in Translation*, he stars as an aging and weary actor navigating the confusion that arises from cultural differences between East and West. In an interview, he commented on how being in Japan in real life made him feel.

—Did you have any "Lost in Translation" moments in Japan?

"I spent ten days in Fukuoka with a friend of mine going to a golf tournament down there. We just had fun down there. They make fun of [people from Tokyo] down in Fukuoka. It's like being in the South. They make fun of Tokyo people like Americans make fun of New Yorkers. They're all so uptight. It was always fun down there. I liked being in a place where no one could understand me, the words. It was also nice to be in a place where people don't recognize you, so you have total freedom to behave and [act out] foul impulses that you can't [control]. I don't know if that's 'lost in translation' or not."

——Bill Murray, interview with *About.com*, 2003

クリント・イーストウッド

クリント・イーストウッド（1930〜）は、アメリカの俳優で、1960年代の「マカロニ・ウェスタン」映画シリーズで有名になりました。その後も、『ダーティハリー』シリーズの主役を演じ、世界的な成功を収めています。それ以来、映画監督、映画プロデューサー、実業家として成功しています。

「私はニューエイジの人間ではありませんが、瞑想は良いものだと信じています。そのため、これまでずっと仏教に惹かれていました。日本を訪れたとき、仏寺に行って瞑想しましたが、価値ある体験になりました」

——クリント・イーストウッド、『デイリー・メイル』紙のインタビュー、2011年1月17日

Clint Eastwood

Clint Eastwood (1930–) is an American actor who became famous in the 1960s in a series of "spaghetti Western" movies. He continued his international success in his central role in the *Dirty Harry* movies. He has since become a successful director, producer, and businessman.

"I'm not a New Age person, but I do believe in meditation, and for that reason I've always liked the Buddhist religion. When I've been to Japan, I've been to Buddhist temples and meditated, and I found that rewarding."

——Clint Eastwood, interview with the *Daily Mail*,
January 17, 2011

トミー・リー・ジョーンズ

トミー・リー・ジョーンズ（1946〜）は、アカデミー賞を受賞した俳優で、映画監督でもあります。おそらく日本で最も愛されているアメリカ人俳優の1人でしょう。たびたび日本のコマーシャルに登場し、約10年間、サントリーの缶コーヒー「BOSS」のコマーシャルに出演しています。第二次世界大戦後の日本の再建を描いた映画『終戦のエンペラー』にマッカーサー元帥の役で出演しています。

「私は世界の劇の歴史という講座を受けて、歌舞伎と能に心を奪われました。能や歌舞伎についての書物を読み、自分で論文を書くうちに好奇心をかき立てられ、日本文化への興味がふくらんでいきました。学べば学ぶほどに、もっと知りたくなったのです」

——トミー・リー・ジョーンズ、東京の大使公邸でのインタビュー、2013年8月1日

Tommy Lee Jones

Oscar-winning actor and director Tommy Lee Jones (1946–) is perhaps one of Japan's most well loved American actors. He often appears in Japanese commercials and has been a spokesperson for Suntory's BOSS Coffee for roughly ten years. He starred as General MacArthur in *Emperor*, a film about Japanese reconstruction after World War II.

"I took a course in the history of world drama and was fascinated with Kabuki and Noh. What I'd read about it and the papers I wrote also intrigued me and my interest in Japanese culture began to grow. The more I learned, the more I wanted to learn."

——Tommy Lee Jones, interview at the Ambassador's Residence in Tokyo, August 1, 2013

ヒュー・グラント

ヒュー・グラント（1960 〜）は、イギリスの俳優で、ロマンチック・コメディの主役として世界中で愛されています。俳優の仕事は好きではないと、しばしば発言していますが、映画賞を受賞しており、『フォー・ウェディング』、『ブリジット・ジョーンズの日記』、『ラブ・アクチュアリー』などの大ヒット映画に出演しています。

「日本の女性たちはいつもぼくの映画を愛してくれました。たとえ、ほかにそんなことをしてくれる人がいないときでもね。1980年代に『モーリス』に出演して以来、日本の若い女性たちから何百通もの手紙をもらっています。間違いなく、彼女たちはぼくにとってかけがえのない存在なのです」

――ヒュー・グラント、『ジャパン・トゥデイ』紙のインタビュー、2010年3月18日

Hugh Grant

British actor Hugh Grant (1960–), internationally loved as the leading man in many romantic comedies, has often said he doesn't like the profession of acting. However, he is an award-winning actor who has starred in smash hits, such as *Four Weddings and a Funeral*, *Bridget Jones's Diary*, and *Love Actually*.

"Japanese women have always loved my films, even when no one else did. Ever since I made 'Maurice' in the 1980s, I've been getting hundreds of letters from Japanese girls. They definitely have a special place in my heart."

——Hugh Grant, interview with *Japan Today*,
March 18, 2010

トム・クルーズ

トム・クルーズ（1962～）は、アメリカの俳優で、1980年代にデビューしました。ロマンチックなコメディやドラマからアクション映画まで様々な作品に出演しています。おそらく『ミッション・インポッシブル』シリーズの主役、イーサン・ハントとして最も知られているでしょう。2003年、『ラストサムライ』でネイサン・オールグレンを演じました。これは日本を舞台にした叙事詩的な映画です。ある情報筋によると、トム・クルーズは大物映画俳優のなかで最も多く日本を訪れているということです。

「ヒロ・サナダ（真田広之）を見てください。ロイヤル・シェイクスピアで演じた大した人物です。日本人として初めてロイヤル・シェイクスピア・カンパニーで演じた俳優です……彼はぼくのところにやって来て、殺陣について助言してくれました。ぼくは互いに励まし合うような環境にいるほうがうまく演じられるし、家族の感覚が好きです。映画を製作しているとき、えー、それはぼくの問題ではないのです。映画自体の問題なのです。ぼくたちが一丸となって一緒に働くことです。ですから、ぼくにとっては、みんなからのそういう種類の支援が本当に大切なのです。それが1つにまとまると……何とも素晴らしい感覚です。そういう支援をケン（渡辺謙）から、関係者みんなから、

Tom Cruise

Tom Cruise (1962–) is an American actor who made his debut in the 1980s. His career encompasses a wide range of work, from romantic comedies and dramas to action movies. He is perhaps best known as Ethan Hunt, the central role in the *Mission: Impossible* series. In 2003, he played Nathan Algren in *The Last Samurai*, an epic film set in Japan. According to some sources, Tom Cruise is known to have paid more visits to Japan than any other major movie star.

"You look at Hiro Sanada, he's someone who was at the Royal Shakespeare. He's the first Japanese actor in the Royal Shakespeare Company. . . . He would come in and work with me on the sword and *kata*. I work better in an environment that is one that is encouraging, and I like a sense of family. When I'm making a film, you know, it's not about me. It's about the movie. It's about us together and working together. So I really depend on that kind of support from everyone, and when it comes together . . . it's a great feeling. I definitely felt that from Ken [Watanabe], from everyone involved. When I'm speaking Japanese, Hiro actually came in and worked

はっきりと感じました。ぼくが日本語で話していると、ヒロが実際にやって来て、日本語のアクセントを教えてくれました。セリフを言っているときやアフレコしているときにね。おかげでアクセントの間違いや言葉の強勢の置き方を直すことができました。つまり、みんなが映画全体を通してそういう種類の支援をしてくれたのです」

——トム・クルーズ、IGNのインタビュー、2003年12月4日

with me on my accent, when I was speaking it and when I was looping it. He helped fix some of the inaccuracies of my accent and the stress on words. So they gave that kind of support throughout the entire film."

———Tom Cruise, interview with *IGN*, December 4, 2003

エドワード・ノートン

エドワード・ノートン（1969〜）は、アカデミー賞候補になったアメリカの俳優で、映画の監督およびプロデューサーでもあります。大学卒業後、祖父の会社のコンサルタントとして大阪に住んで働いていたことがあります。日本語が堪能で、東日本大震災後に日本に対して見舞いの言葉を述べました。

「私は1990年に大阪に住んでいて、そこにたくさんの友人がいます。日本人のすべてのきょうだいに愛と支援を送ります。ガンバッテ！」

——エドワード・ノートン、ツイッター、2011年3月14日

Edward Norton

Edward Norton (1969–) is an Academy Award–nominated American actor who has also directed and produced films. Norton lived and worked in Osaka after his college years as a consultant for his grandfather's company. He speaks Japanese well and expressed sympathy for Japan after the Tohoku earthquake and tsunami.

"I lived in Osaka, Japan in 1990 and have many friends there. Sending love and support to all Nihonzin brothers and sisters. *Ganbatte!*"

——Edward Norton, Twitter, March 14, 2011

第8章
スポーツ選手とスタッフ

Chapter 8
Athletes and Sports Professionals

Derek Jeter
Cristiano Ronaldo dos Santos Aveiro
Muhammad Ali
Barry Bonds
Apolo Ohno
Kristi Yamaguchi
Rob Manfred

デレク・ジーター

デレク・ジーター（1974〜）は、アメリカの野球選手で、ニューヨーク・ヤンキースで20シーズンプレイしました。多くのヤンキース記録と大リーグ記録を保持し、ヤンキースの5回のワールドシリーズ優勝に貢献しました。チームメートの松井秀喜の親友でした。松井はヤンキースに7シーズン所属し、外野手や指名打者としても活躍しました。松井が野球を引退するとき、ジーターは松井のことを「ぼくの大好きなチームメートの1人」と呼び、賛辞を送りました。

「彼はプロだよ。毎日、試合に出ていた。最も偉大なのは、けっして言い訳をしなかったことだ。怪我のことを口にしたことはなかったし、怪我を言い訳にしなかった。いつも球場に行き、プレイしていた。これは野球選手として、尊敬に値することだ」

——デレク・ジーター、松井秀喜を語る、『ジャーナル・ニュース』紙、LoHudヤンキース・ブログから引用、2013年7月

Derek Jeter

Derek Jeter (1974–) is an American baseball player who played for the New York Yankees for twenty seasons. He holds many Yankees and Major League Baseball records and has helped the Yankees win five World Series. He became close friends with teammate Hideki Matsui, who was an outfielder and designated hitter of the Yankees for seven seasons. Upon Matsui's retirement from baseball, Jeter called Matsui "one of my favorite teammates" and had many nice things to say about him.

"He was a professional. He played every day. The biggest thing is he never made excuses. He never talked about injuries; he never used injuries as an excuse. He went out there and played. As players, you appreciate that."

——Derek Jeter on Hideki Matsui, quoted by the LoHud Yankees Blog of
The Journal News, July 2013

クリスティアーノ・ロナウド・ドス・サントス・アヴェイロ

クリスティアーノ・ロナウド・ドス・サントス・アヴェイロ（1985〜）は、一般にはクリスティアーノ・ロナウドとして知られているポルトガルのサッカー選手です。多くの人が世界で最も偉大な選手だと考えています。幼少のころにサッカーを始め、小さいときから才能豊かな選手として目立っていました。2003年にプロになり、ポルトガル人として初めてマンチェスター・ユナイテッドの選手になりました。2009年にレアル・マドリードに移籍し、現在も所属しています。

「ぼくにとって日本は素晴らしい国です。前にも言いましたが、ぼくの意見では、おそらくアジアで最高の国の1つだと思います。以前にもマンチェスター・ユナイテッドの選手として日本に来たことがあり、10日間、滞在しました。町は素晴らしいです。きれいで汚れていません。もちろん、人々はとても親切です。すごく熱狂的ですしね」

——クリスティアーノ・ロナウド、美容用品メーカーMTGのスポークスパーソンとしてファンにインタビュー、日本のテレビで放送、2014年

Cristiano Ronaldo dos Santos Aveiro

Cristiano Ronaldo dos Santos Aveiro (1985–), popularly known as Cristiano Ronaldo, is a Portuguese soccer player who is thought by many to be the greatest player in the world. He began playing soccer as a child and stood out at an early age as a brilliant player. He went professional in 2003, when he became the first-ever Portuguese player to join Manchester United. In 2009, he joined Real Madrid, where he currently plays.

"Japan for me is a fantastic country. As I said before, it's probably one of the best in Asia, in my opinion. I had an opportunity to be here before with Manchester United and we stayed here for ten days, and the city is fantastic. It's a very clean city. The people, of course, are very nice. They are very fanatic."

——Cristiano Ronaldo, interview with a fan as a spokesperson for beauty product maker MTG, aired on Japanese television in 2014

モハメド・アリ

モハメド・アリ（1942〜）は、史上最強の偉大なプロボクサーの1人として知られています。61試合のうち勝ちが56という輝かしい戦績を残しました。1964年に宗教組織「ネーション・オブ・イスラム」に入信し、カシアス・クレイからモハメド・アリに改名して、宗教の自由を表明する文化的な名士になりました。1976年、プロレスラーのアントニオ・猪木と対戦するために来日しました。試合前に、猪木を題材にしてちょっとした曲を作曲し、ピアノを弾きながら歌いました。

「俺は猪木をつぶす、あいつは倒れる！
俺こそ本物の世界チャンピオン
猪木をつぶす、あいつは倒れる！
だって俺は最強だからね
おい、ノックアウトすると猪木に言ってくれ！
おい、ノックアウトすると猪木に言ってくれ！
教えてやるよ、あいつをいつノックアウトするか
あいつは倒れる！　8ラウンドでおしまいさ」

——モハメド・アリ、日本のテレビで放送、1976年

Muhammad Ali

Muhammad Ali (1942–) is considered one of the greatest professional boxers of all time. His boxing record boasts 56 wins out of 61 total fights. He became a cultural figure representing religious freedom when he joined the Nation of Islam in 1964 and changed his given name, Cassius Clay, to Muhammad Ali. In 1976, Ali traveled to Japan to fight martial artist Antonio Inoki. Before the match, Ali composed a little song about Inoki, which he sang while playing the piano:

"I will destroy him, Inoki must fall!
I am the real world champion.
I shall destroy him, Inoki must fall!
Because I'm the greatest in the world.
Hey, tell Inoki I'm going to knock him out!
Hey, tell Inoki I'm going to knock him out!
Well, let me tell you just how I'm going to knock him out.
He must fall! He must fall in Round 8."

———Muhammad Ali, broadcast on Japanese television, 1976

バリー・ボンズ

バリー・ボンズ（1964～）は、史上最高の野球選手の1人とみなされ、メジャーリーグで22シーズン活躍しました。ボンズは、1シーズンの最多ホームラン、最多通算ホームランなど多くの記録を保持していますが、2007年に浮上したステロイド疑惑で、彼のスポーツマン精神と誠実な人柄が問われることになりました。その後の裁判で、司法妨害で有罪になりましたが、この有罪判決は2015年に翻されました。2002年にはオールスターゲームのために来日し、日本で楽しいひとときを過ごしました。

「とても楽しい。アメリカにいるときとはまったく違うんだ。これほどのチームでこんな選手たちと試合できるなんてね。だれにとっても夢だね。アメリカ人としてこんなチームにいられるなんて、本当にわくわくするよ。

このツアーには初めてトレーナーを連れて来た。彼はいつもこう言うんだ。『日本はまったく違っている。みんなとても親切だ。そしてどの人も、こんにちは、こんにちはと、挨拶してくれる。こんな風に扱われたら、だれでも簡単に親切な人になれるよ』ってね」

——バリー・ボンズ、日本でオールスター戦に出場、ESPN（娯楽スポーツテレビ放送ネットワーク）のインタビュー、2002年

Barry Bonds

Barry Bonds (1964–), considered one of the greatest baseball players of all time, played twenty-two seasons in Major League Baseball. Although Bonds holds many records, such as most home runs in a season and most career home runs, Bonds's sportsmanship and integrity was questioned in a steroids scandal that surfaced in 2007. In a trial that followed, he was found guilty of obstruction of justice, but this conviction was overturned in 2015. In 2002, Bonds traveled to Japan on an All-Star tour and enjoyed his time in the country.

"This is fun. It's a whole lot different than in the States. You get to play on a team like this with players like these? It's everyone's dream. It's exciting as an American to be on a team like this.

"I brought my trainer along on the trip for the first time and he keeps saying, 'Japan is so different. Everyone is so nice. They all say, 'Hi, Hi, Hi.' It's easy to become a nice person when you're treated like that."

——Barry Bonds on playing an All-Star tour in Japan, interview with ESPN, 2002

アポロ・オーノ

アポロ・オーノ（1982～）は、アメリカのスピードスケート選手で、3度の冬季オリンピックで8個のメダルを獲得しました。さらに、様々な世界選手権大会で8個のメダルを獲得しています。日本人の父、大野幸（おおの・ゆき）から訓練を受けたため、アポロは日本の国と国民に対してしばしば感謝の意と懸念を示しています。

「（日本の）食べ物は信じられないほど素晴らしい。たとえ寿司がきらいでもね！ 日本人は質に対してこだわりがあって、それが料理法となると——ものすごく真剣なんだ。もし、フランス菓子やイタリア料理を食べたくてたまらなくなったら——日本人の準備、味覚、きれい好き、そしてもちろん、もてなしの精神にはうならされるよ。1つ忠告するとすれば——日本語が話せて、東京周辺の地域を熟知した人と出かけること。そうすれば一風変わったところに行けるよ」

——アポロ・オーノ、『USAトゥデイ』紙のインタビュー、2009年9月

Apolo Ohno

Apolo Ohno (1982–) is an American speed skater who has won eight Olympic medals over three Winter Olympics. He has also won eight gold medals at various world championships. Trained by his Japanese-born father, Yuki Ohno, Apolo has often expressed an appreciation and concern for the nation and people of Japan.

"The food [in Japan] is incredible, even if you do not like sushi! The Japanese have acquired a dedication towards quality and when it comes to cuisine—they take (it) extremely seriously. If you crave a French pastry, or Italian food—the Japanese will wow you on their preparation, taste, cleanliness and, of course, hospitality. If I would have one recommendation: Go with someone who speaks Japanese and is familiar with the areas surrounding Tokyo so that you will go off the beaten path."

——Apolo Ohno, interview with *USA Today*, September 2009

クリスティー・ヤマグチ

クリスティー・ヤマグチ（1971〜）は、日系アメリカ人のフィギュアスケート選手で、1992年に開催された冬季オリンピックの女子シングルで金メダルを獲得しました。そのほかにも多くの国内および国際選手権で活躍しました。2005年には合衆国オリンピックの殿堂入りを果たしました。2010年のテレビインタビューで、ティーンエイジャーとして初めて先祖の国を訪れたときの日本の印象を次のように語っています。

「最初に行ったのが東京だった。そこではまるで科学技術が通りを歩いているようで感動したわ……いたるところでネオンが輝き、それに、電子技術が進んでいた――ソニーのウォークマンやそんなものすべてが発表されたばかりだったのね。だから、私は科学技術に魅せられたの。あんなに大勢の人が密集している区域なのに、恐ろしいほど整然としていたことを覚えているわ。実際、通りにはゴミ1つ落ちていなかった。あんな狭い区域に住んでいる人の数を考えると、信じられないほどきちんとしていて、きれいだった。忘れられない思い出ね」

――クリスティー・ヤマグチ、PBS『フェイス・オブ・アメリカ』でヘンリー・ルイス・ゲイツ・ジュニアとのインタビュー、2010年

Kristi Yamaguchi

Kristi Yamaguchi (1971–) is a Japanese American figure skater who won the gold medal in ladies' singles skating at the 1992 Olympic Winter Games. She went on to win numerous other national and international titles and championships. She was inducted into the U.S. Olympic Hall of Fame in 2005. In a television interview in 2010, she recalled her impressions of Japan when she first visited her ancestral home as a teenager.

"I think my first trip to Japan was to Tokyo, and I think I was impressed by the technology walking down the street. . . . seeing the neon lights everywhere and, you know, the electronic advancements they had—I think they had just come out with the Sony Walkman and all of that, so I think the technology side fascinated me. I think the fact that there were so many people in a condensed area and yet it was amazingly orderly. I mean, you never saw a piece of garbage on the street; it was just incredibly neat and clean for the number of people that were living in such a small area. I do remember that."

——Kristi Yamaguchi, interview with *Faces of America with Henry Louis Gates, Jr.*, PBS, 2010

ロブ・マンフレッド

ロブ・マンフレッド（1958〜）は、2015年1月に第10代メジャーリーグコミッショナーに任命されました。1987年からMLBで働き始め、1998年にMLBの経済およびリーグ部門の取締副社長になりました。彼は明敏な弁護士で実業家でもあり、2014年後半に、2016年の開幕戦は日本で行いたいと発表しました。

「野球ファンが私たちの試合を生で見る機会を得ることはとても重要だと考えています。これは野球の国際化にとって、またとない手段でしょう。このことは特に日本について言えます。というのも野球は競争の激しいスポーツになったからです。今では日本の野球チームはとても強くなっていますので、私たちが来日したときには拮抗したシリーズが見られるでしょう」

——ロブ・マンフレッド、『読売新聞』のインタビュー、2014年11月23日

Rob Manfred

In January 2015, Rob Manfred (1958–) was appointed the tenth Commissioner of Baseball. He started working with Major League Baseball (MLB) in 1987, and in 1998 he became the Executive Vice President of Economics and League Affairs for MLB. He is an astute lawyer and businessman, and in late 2014, he said 2016 might see an opening series in Japan.

"We think that it's very important for fans to have an opportunity to see our product live. It really is the best vehicle that we have for the internationalization of the game. It's particularly true in Japan, because the baseball has become so competitive. The Japanese teams have become so strong now, you get a very competitive series when we come here."

——Rob Manfred, *Yomiuri Shimbun* interview, November 23, 2014

編集部よりのあとがき

　本書に収録した著名人のコメントのうち、とくに歴史上のコメントをどう捉えるかについては、いろいろな感想を持った読者の方々がいるのではないでしょうか。

　わたしたちが、ここで知っておかなければならないことは、「歴史上のコメントのトリック」ということです。

　人類は、歴史上、さまざまな利害関係の中で文明を成長させてきました。

　例えば、ある地域がある国家の植民地として圧政に苦しんでいたとします。すると、植民地の人々はその国家を攻撃する他の国の動きを支援します。

　その時に、他の国の行為が歴史的にどう評価されているかとは全く別の判断が植民地の人々によってなされることがあるのです。

　実例でみてみましょう。アメリカは、イギリスから独立するときに、イギリスのライバルであったフランスの支援を確保します。しかし、当のフランスはブルボン王朝が君臨する、イギリスよりも民主化の遅れた国家でした。

　アメリカ独立の英雄たちは、イギリスの圧政からの解放と「自由」をテーマに革命を起こします。つまり、当時のフランスの国是とは相容れないはずの思想で、行動を起こしたのですが、政策としては親フランスの姿勢を貫くのです。

　もう一つの事例としてウクライナのケースを紹介しましょう。

　ウクライナは伝統的にロシア（あるいはソ連）の影響下にあって、常に独立の機運がありました。だからこそ、独立派の人々の中には、ナチスドイツに協力した人もいたのです。そうした人々は、当時ナチスドイツ寄りのコメントを発表して、ソ連に対峙していました。

　次にアジアに目を向けましょう。

　本書には、イギリスの植民地であったインドの独立を指揮したガンディーのコメントを掲載していますが、その盟友のネルーなどは、日本が西欧列強と比肩するまでに台頭してきたことを、胸を躍らせて観察していたと聞いています。東京裁判で、ただ一人

日本のA級戦犯を裁くことに消極的だったことで知られるインド出身の裁判官ラダ・ビノード・パールのコメントは、専門的すぎるので本書では掲載しませんでしたが、20世紀の複雑な国際関係を理解した上でそれを読み込むと、その真価がみえてくるのです。

　当然、西欧社会の中にも、19世紀から20世紀にかけての、いわゆる西欧列強の植民地主義や西欧偏重の文明観などに疑問をもっていた人々も多くいました。

　今からみれば、そうした人々は未来志向で極めてリベラルな視点を持った人々です。彼らの中には、アジアで力を蓄えてきた日本について、それを賞賛する気持ちがあったのも事実です。例えば、本書にて取り上げたチョムスキーの真珠湾攻撃へのコメントなどは、西欧の識者の考え方の代表ともいえるのではないでしょうか。しかし、日本の侵略行為でアジアの多くの国々が災禍を被ったのもまた現実です。

　そのときの立場や、状況によって、人々のコメントはさまざまに解釈され、利用されます。それが、誤解を生むこともあれば、誤って利用されることもあるのです。「歴史上のコメントのトリック」とは、そうした人々のコメントの持つ背景の複雑さを意味しているのです。

　日本人がそうしたコメントを読むときに、それを文字通りにとって判断すると、ここに記したトリックにひっかかり、誤解をしてしまうことがあります。

　例えば毛沢東が、戦前の日本の中国での侵略行為について、肯定するかのようなコメントをしていることを本書では紹介しています。これは、おそらく日中戦争を戦った毛沢東の皮肉であるとともに、大きな目でみれば、阿片戦争以来西欧列強の侵略に晒されていた中国が、日本という西欧をも敵にしている相手と戦ったことで、最終的に西欧社会の侵略行為をも克服できたという含みがあることを忘れてはなりません。

　本書に紹介するコメントをどのように読み込んでゆくか……歴史の1ページ1ページの背景を振り返りながら、それを洞察する楽しみを味わっていただければ幸いです。

[対訳ニッポン双書]
ニッポン感想記
Japan through the World's Eyes

2015年9月5日　第1刷発行

著　者　ニーナ・ウェグナー

訳　者　宇野 葉子

発行者　浦　　晋 亮

発行所　IBCパブリッシング株式会社
　　　　〒162-0804 東京都新宿区中里町29番3号 菱秀神楽坂ビル9F
　　　　Tel. 03-3513-4511　Fax. 03-3513-4512
　　　　www.ibcpub.co.jp

印刷所　株式会社シナノパブリッシングプレス

© IBC パブリッシング 2015
Printed in Japan

落丁本・乱丁本は、小社宛にお送りください。送料小社負担にてお取り替えいたします。
本書の無断複写（コピー）は著作権法上での例外を除き禁じられています。

ISBN978-4-7946-0371-5